Chinese State Owned Enterprises and EU Merger Control

This book analyzes the specifics of corporate governance of China's State Owned Enterprises (SOEs) and their assessment under EU merger control, which is reflected in the EU Commission's screening of the notified economic concentrations.

Guided by 'go global' policy and the Belt and Road Initiative, Chinese SOEs have expanded their global presence considerably. Driven by the need to acquire cutting-edge technologies and other industrial policy considerations, Chinese SOEs have engaged in a series of corporate acquisitions in Europe. The main objective of this book is to demonstrate the conceptual and regulatory challenges of applying traditional merger assessment tools in cases involving Chinese SOEs due to the specifics in their corporate governance and the regulatory framework under which they operate in China. The book also explores the connection between the challenges experienced by the merger control regimes in the EU and the recent introduction of the EU foreign direct investment screening framework followed by a proposal concerning foreign subsidies.

The book will be a useful guide for academics and researchers in the fields of law, international relations, political science, and political economy; legal practitioners dealing with cross-border mergers and acquisitions; national competition authorities and other public bodies carrying out merger control; policy makers, government officials, and diplomats in China and the EU engaged in bilateral economic relations.

Alexandr Svetlicinii is an associate professor at the University of Macau, Faculty of Law, where he also serves as Program Coordinator of the Master of International Business Law in English Language. Prior to joining the University of Macau, Dr. Svetlicinii was a senior researcher at the Jean Monnet Chair of European Law at the Tallinn Law School, Tallinn University of Technology, in Estonia. In addition to his academic work, Dr. Svetlicinii served as the Non-Governmental Advisor to the International Competition Network (working group Mergers) and acted as a consultant in a number of research projects of the European Commission.

Chinese State Owned Enterprises and EU Merger Control

Alexandr Svetlicinii

LONDON AND NEW YORK

First published 2021
by Routledge
2 Park Square, Milton Park, Abingdon, Oxon OX14 4RN

and by Routledge
52 Vanderbilt Avenue, New York, NY 10017

Routledge is an imprint of the Taylor & Francis Group, an informa business

British Library Cataloguing-in-Publication Data
A catalogue record for this book is available from the British Library

Library of Congress Cataloging-in-Publication Data
A catalog record for this book has been requested

ISBN: 978-0-367-51320-7 (hbk)
ISBN: 978-0-367-51325-2 (pbk)
ISBN: 978-1-003-05335-4 (ebk)

Typeset in Times New Roman
by Apex CoVantage, LLC

Contents

Preface and acknowledgments

The research for this book benefited from discussions and feedback received at various academic events where I had an opportunity to present the preliminary findings: the Law & Society Annual Meeting 'Dignity' at the Hyatt Regency Washington on Capitol Hill, Washington, D.C. (United States) on 31 May 2019; the International Conference of the Jean Monnet Network 'EU-China Legal and Judicial Cooperation' (EUPLANT) 'The Internationalisation of EU Law and EU-China Relations' at Queen Mary University of London (United Kingdom) on 11 June 2019 (with special thanks to Matthieu Burnay); the 14th Annual Conference of the Academic Society for Competition Law 'Challenges to Assumptions at the Basis of Competition Law' at Aix Marseille University, Aix-en-Provence (France) on 27 June 2019; the Asian Society of International Law 7th Biennial Conference 'Rethinking International Law: Finding Common Solutions to Contemporary Civilization Issues from an Asian Perspective' at the Novotel Manila Araneta Center, Manila (Philippines) on 23 August 2019; the 6th Competition Law and Policy Conference in Memory of Dr. Vedran Šoljan 'Challenges to the Enforcement of Competition Rules in Central and Eastern Europe' at the University of Zagreb, Faculty of Economics and Business, Zagreb (Croatia) on 12 December 2019 (with special thanks to Jasminka Pecotić Kaufman); the Asian Law and Society Association 4th Annual Meeting 'Expanding Asia: Changing Law and Social Justice' at Osaka University, Osaka (Japan) on 14 December 2019; the Workshop of the 'Innovation Kaken' Project at the Kobe University School of Law, Kobe (Japan) (with special thanks to Masako Wakui and Thomas Cheng) on 21 December 2019; the 15th Annual (Virtual) Conference of the Academic Society for Competition Law on 27 June 2020; the China International Business and Economic Law (CIBEL) Centre Global Network Virtual Conference, Online Panel 'The Pandemic and Investment Law: A Good or Bad Coincidence?' on 6 August 2020; the Online Workshop on European Legal Studies, Swedish Network for European Legal Studies on 20 August 2020 (with special thanks to Vladimir

Bastidas and Eva Storskrubb); the Online Workshop of the European Society of International Law, International Economic Law Interest Group 'International Economic Law between Emergencies and Reforms' on 9 September 2020; the 16th ALIN International Conference 'Laws for Fading Borders in Asia' of the Korea Legislation Research Institute on 18 September 2020 (with special thanks to Hye-Shin Cho); the Academic Society for Competition Law, Asia and Eurasia Virtual Regional Workshop 'Current Issues in Antitrust in Asia and Eurasia' on 10 October 2020 (with special thanks to Masako Wakui, Thomas Cheng, Sandra Marco Colino).

Many other individuals deserve an acknowledgment for their friendship and collaboration in this research project, which benefited from their feedback and support in publicizing the research findings: Alexey G. Barabashev, Maciej Bernatt, Julien Chaisse, Stephen Minas, Rostam J. Neuwirth, Vassilis Ntousas, Sofia Pais, Su Xueji, Anne Tercinet, and Thomas Weck.

I am thankful to Li Chen, Zhang Juanjuan, Ina Virtosu, Guo Xinyan, Li Yimo, Yin Yanni and Cai Zhuohao for their research assistance. Special thanks go to Alison Kirk for patiently guiding me through the publication process. I am also grateful to the anonymous peer reviewers for their constructive criticism, as well as to the language proofreaders who helped improve the quality of the work.

The author's research has been supported by the Asia Europe Comparative Studies Research Project – IEEM Academic Research Grant 2019 awarded by the Institute of European Studies of Macau.

Macao SAR (China)
Alexandr Svetlicinii
11 October 2020

Abbreviations

AML	anti-monopoly law
AVIC	Aviation Industry Corporation of China
CCPIA	China Crop Protection Industry Association
CEO	chief executive officer
CGN	China General Nuclear Power Corporation
CJEU	Court of Justice of the European Union
CNAC	China National Agrochemical Corporation
CNCE	China National Chemical Equipment Co. Ltd
CNIA	China Nuclear Industry Alliance
CNOOC	China National Offshore Oil Corporation
CNPC	China National Petroleum Corporation
CNRC	China National Tyre & Rubber Co. Ltd
CNY	Chinese yuan
CPC	Communist Party of China
EDF	Electricité de France S.A.
EEA	European Economic Area
EU	European Union
EUMR	EU Merger Regulation
EUR	euro
FDI	foreign direct investment
MOFCOM	Ministry of Commerce
NCA	national competition authority
NDRC	National Development and Reform Commission
NOC	national oil company
NSC	National Supervisory Commission
OECD	Organisation for Economic Co-operation and Development
PRC	People's Republic of China
SAMR	State Administration for Market Regulation
SASAC	State-Owned Assets Supervision and Administration Commission

SHIG	Shandong Heavy Industry Group Co. Ltd
SME	small or medium-sized enterprise
SOE	state owned enterprise
SoFFin	*Sonderfonds Finanzmarktstabilisierung*
TEC	Treaty Establishing the European Community
TFEU	Treaty on the Functioning of the European Union
UK	United Kingdom of Great Britain and Northern Ireland
UOKiK	*Urząd Ochrony Konkurencji i Konsumentów*
US	United States of America

1 State owned enterprises under the EU merger control

1.1 State owned enterprise as 'undertaking' or 'person' under the EU merger control

The notion of undertaking is a relative concept in the sense that a given entity might be regarded as an undertaking for one part of its activities while the rest fall outside the competition rules.[1]

Article 345 of the Treaty on the Functioning of the European Union (TFEU) (ex-Article 295 TEC) provides that the EU law should not prejudice 'the rules in Member States governing the system of property ownership', which establishes a principle of neutrality or non-discrimination between state owned and privately owned companies. According to the Organisation for Economic Co-operation and Development (OECD), competition law is 'a powerful tool to level the playing field by addressing competition concerns stemming from SOE conduct, provided such conduct amounts to an abuse of dominance, cartel participation, or is subject to merger control'.[2] When it comes to the regulatory sphere of competition law, including merger control, the SOEs are viewed as market players along with the other types of businesses. In order to maintain the level playing field among various types of market players, the EU and its Member States adhere to the principle of competitive neutrality in their regulatory treatment of the SOEs.[3] According to the Commission,

---

1 Case C-475/99 *Ambulanz Glockner v Landkreis Südwestpfalz* [2001] ECR I-08089 Opinion of AG Jacobs, para 72.
2 Organisation for Economic Co-Operation and Development, 'Governments as Competitors in the Global Marketplace: Options for Ensuring a Level Playing Field' (2016) <http://e15initiative.org/publications/governments-as-competitors-in-the-global-marketplace-options-for-ensuring-a-level-playing-field/> accessed 31 July 2020, 8.
3 See Organisation for Economic Co-Operation and Development, 'Ownership and Governance of State-Owned Enterprises: A Compendium of National Practices' (2018) <www.oecd.

if it was allowed to treat state-owned undertakings more favourably than other enterprises, removing the level playing field that should be the characteristic of free competition, the competitive process and the long-term goal of one European integrated market could be considerably damaged.[4]

The principle of competitive neutrality is also enshrined in the EU Merger Regulation (EUMR), which declares that the 'arrangements to be introduced for the control of concentrations should . . . respect the principle of non-discrimination between the public and the private sectors'.[5]

Following the principle of competitive neutrality, the SOEs do not have any specific regulatory treatment under the EUMR, and their mergers and acquisitions falling under the ambit of EUMR have to pass through the same procedural steps and substantive assessment standards. It is therefore expected that the state ownership of a company does not have to be acknowledged in the Commission's merger decisions, especially when it does not affect the competitive assessment of the notified concentration. For example, in the *Gaz de France/Ruhrgas/Slovensky* merger case, the French SOE Gaz de France is referred to as 'integrated gas company mainly active in France at all levels of distribution and supply'. At the same time, the Commission acknowledged the SOE status of Slovak Gas Industry (*Slovenský plynárenský priemysel* or SPP), which at the time of transaction was 'currently a fully state-owned company'.[6]

The understanding of the status of SOEs under the EU merger control regime should commence from the definition of the term 'undertaking', which is the primary subject of regulation under the EUMR and under EU competition law in general. Although the EUMR on numerous occasions uses the term 'undertakings concerned', it does not provide a definition of this term. Although the same concept appears in the fundamental rules of the EU competition law – Articles 101 and 102 TFEU – the Treaty does not define this concept either. Article 101 TFEU, which prohibits anti-competitive collusion refers to 'agreements between undertakings' and 'decisions by associations of undertakings'. Article 102 TFEU, which targets unilateral

org/corporate/Ownership-and-Governance-of-State-Owned-Enterprises-A-Compendium-of-National-Practices.pdf> accessed 31 July 2020, 46.

4 Organisation for Economic Co-Operation and Development, 'State Owned Enterprises and the Principle of Competitive Neutrality' (2009) DAF/COMP(2009)37 <www.oecd.org/daf/competition/46734249.pdf> accessed 31 July 2020, 243.

5 Council Regulation (EC) No 139/2004 of 20 January 2004 on the control of concentrations between undertakings (EUMR), OJ L24/1, 29 January 2004, recital 22.

6 *Gaz de France/Ruhrgas/Slovensky* (Case COMP/M.2791) [2002] OJ L154/08, decision of 6 June 2002, paras 3, 6.

anti-competitive conduct, refers to 'abuse by one or more undertakings of a dominant position'. As a result, the meaning of this term has been largely defined through the two main lines of case law: one dealing with concerted conduct under Article 101 TFEU, another with the attribution of liability for competition law infringements.[7]

In relation to Article 101 TFEU, the 'undertaking' must possess an autonomy in its decision making because the anti-competitive agreements, prohibited by the said provision, should be concluded by the economically independent entities, which is not the case with a parent company and its subsidiary.[8] For instance, if

> the subsidiary, although having a separate legal personality, does not freely determine its conduct on the market but carries out the instructions given to it directly or indirectly by the parent company by which it is wholly controlled [Article 101(1) TFEU], does not apply to the relationship between the subsidiary and the parent company with which it forms an economic unit.[9]

Or, as summarized by Whish,

> the crucial question is whether parties to an agreement are independent in their decision-making or whether one has sufficient control over the affairs of the other than the latter does not enjoy 'real autonomy' in determining its course of action on the market.[10]

The determination of the 'single economic unit' has been further developed in the case law of the Court of Justice of the European Union (CJEU)

7 See Alison Jones, 'The Boundaries of an Undertaking in EU Competition Law' (2012) 8 *European Competition Journal* 301, 303.
8 See Alexandr Svetlicinii, 'The Competition Authority of Bosnia & Herzegovina Follows EU Competition Law Standards and Rejects an Anticompetitive Agreement Complaint in Relation to Affiliated Companies Being Part of A "Single Economic Entity" (*Elektrokontakt / Elektroprivreda / Eldis-Tehnika*)' (2011) e-Competitions February 2011, Art. N° 36981 <www.concurrences.com/en/bulletin/news-issues/february-2011/the-competition-authority-of-bosnia-herzegovina-follows-eu-competition-law-en> accessed 31 July 2020; Alexandr Svetlicinii, 'The Court of Bosnia and Herzegovina Quashes the No-Infringement Decision of the Competition Authority Based on the Concept of "Single Economic Entity" (*Elektrokontakt*)' (2014) e-Competitions January 2014, Art. N° 64923 <www.concurrences.com/en/bulletin/news-issues/january-2014/the-court-of-bosnia-and-herzegovina-quashes-the-no-infringement-decision-of-the-en> accessed 31 July 2020.
9 Case C-73/95 P *Viho Europe BV v Commission* [1996] ECR I-05457, judgment of 24 October 1996, para 51.
10 Richard Whish, *Competition Law* (Oxford University Press 2003), 88–89.

dealing with attribution of liability for competition law infringements. The court in Luxembourg explained that

> it is settled case-law that anti-competitive conduct of an undertaking can be attributed to another undertaking where it has not decided independently upon its own conduct on the market, but carried out, in all materials respects, the instructions given to it by that other undertaking, having regard in particular to the economic and legal links between them.[11]

For example, the General Court has confirmed the infringement decision for abuse of dominant position against Slovak Telekom, which also included a fine imposed on its parent company – Deutsche Telekom – which engaged in frequent exchanges of information and issued instructions to the board of its subsidiary.[12] Apart from establishing a rebuttable presumption of control based on majority shareholding, the CJEU has continuously increased the flexibility of the criteria taken into account when establishing the 'single economic unit' in individual cases.[13]

Starting from its early case law, the CJEU has continuously emphasized the economic rationale of the term 'undertaking' by explaining that 'the concept of an undertaking encompasses every entity engaged in an economic activity regardless of the legal status of the entity and the way in which it is financed'.[14] The substance of economic activity is the supply/purchase of goods/services on the market.[15] This functional approach led to the situation where the same entity can be viewed as 'undertaking' in relation to its economic activity, while its public interest activity would fall outside the scope of competitive law enforcement. For example, in *SELEX Sistemi Integrati*

---

11 Case C-294/98 P *Metsä-Serla Oyj, UPM-Kymmene Oyj, Tamrock Oy and Kyro Oyj Abp v Commission* [2000] ECR I-10065, judgment of 16 November 2000, para 27.

12 Case T-827/14 *Deutsche Telekom AG v Commission* [2018] ECR, judgment of 13 December 2018. See Francesco Liberatore, 'Slovak Telekom/Deutsche Telekom AG: The Interplay between EU Competition Law and Sector-Specific Rules in the Electronic Communications Sector' (2019) 40 *European Competition Law Review* 502.

13 See Alexandr Svetlicinii, 'Who Is to Blame? Liability of "Economic Units" for Infringement of EU Competition Law' (2011) 2 *European Law Reporter* 52; Christian Kerstling, 'Liability of Sister Companies and Subsidiaries in European Competition Law' (2020) 41 *European Competition Law Review* 125; Duncan Sinclair, '"Undertakings" in Competition Law at the Public-Private Interface: An Unhealthy Situation' (2014) 35 *European Competition Law Review* 161.

14 Case C-41/90 *Höfner and Elser v Macrotron GmbH* [1991] ECR I-01979, judgment of 23 April 1991, para 21.

15 Case C-118/85 *Commission v Italy* [1987] ECR 02599, judgment of 16 June 1987, para 7.

SpA v Commission litigation, the CJEU has examined various activities of the Eurocontrol, an international organization entrusted with fostering cooperation between its member states in the field of air navigation and air traffic management.[16] The case confirmed application of competition law to the activities of public bodies and international organizations to the extent they engage in economic activity and can be regarded as 'undertakings'.[17] At the same time, Article 106 TFEU mandates that the application of competition law to the 'undertakings entrusted with the operation of services of general economic interest or having the character of a revenue-producing monopoly' should 'not obstruct the performance, in law or in fact, of the particular tasks assigned to them'. The CJEU has clarified that the general economic interest exception should apply in cases where the restriction of competition is necessary for the undertaking to provide the service of general economic interest under economically viable conditions.[18]

Under the EUMR, the meaning of the term 'undertaking concerned' is linked to the underlying transaction in which the said undertaking is engaged. Thus, 'the undertakings concerned are, broadly speaking, the actors in the transaction in so far as they are the merging, or acquiring and acquired parties'.[19] As a result, the primary focus of attention under the merger control regime was directed at the relationships between undertakings rather than the commercial nature of their activities. For example, in the *Kali-Salz/MdK/Treuhand* case, the Commission considered the Treuhandanstalt (Treuhand), 'an institution incorporated under public law whose task is to restructure the former GDR's State-owned enterprises so as to make them competitive and then to privatize them',[20] as an undertaking, which sought

16 Case C-113/07 P *SELEX Sistemi Integrati SpA v Commission* [2009] ECR I-02207, judgment of 26 March 2009. See Julian Nowag, 'SELEX Sistemi Integrati SpA v Commission of the European Communities (C-113/07 P) [2009] E.C.R. I-2207: Redefining the Boundaries between Undertaking and the Exercise of Public Authority' (2010) 31 *European Competition Law Review* 483.

17 See Alexandr Svetlicinii, 'Back to the Basics: Concepts of Undertaking and Economic Activity in the SELEX Judgment' (2009) 12 *European Law Reporter* 422.

18 See Case C-157/94 *Commission v Netherlands* [1997] ECR I-05699, judgment of 23 October 1997; Case C-158/94 *Commission v Italy* [1997] ECR I-05789, judgment of 23 October 1997; Case C-159/94 *Commission v France* [1997] ECR I-05815, judgment of 23 October 1997.

19 Commission Notice on the concept of undertakings concerned under Council Regulation (EEC) No 4064/89 on the control of concentrations between undertakings, OJ C66/14, 2 March 1998, para 3.

20 *Kali-Salz/MdK/Treuhand* (Case IV/M.308) Decision 94/449/EC [1993] OJ L184/38, para 4. See Nicole Hacker, 'The EU Court of Justice Annuls for the First Time a Commission's Decision under the Merger Regulation (*Kali+Salz / MDK / Deutsche Treuhand*)'

to establish a joint venture with another undertaking (Kali-Salz, a subsidiary of the chemicals group BASF).

Another specific term that is used to designate the parties in the concentration under the EUMR is the term 'person'. This term has a broader scope than 'undertaking' because it encompasses any natural or legal persons or entities that exercise or acquire control over an undertaking. The Jurisdictional Notice further elaborates that the 'term "person" in this context extends to public bodies and private entities, as well as natural persons'.[21] Thus, the rights of control over an undertaking and their exercise will qualify a natural or legal person as 'person concerned' under the EUMR. As a result, even the state in relation to the SOEs it controls can be regarded as 'person', whereas the SOEs could be viewed as 'undertakings concerned'. For example, in the *Air France/Sabena* merger case, the Belgian State transferred certain rights in its airline Sabena to the French national flag carrier Air France, which made Sabena a joint venture between the two controlling 'persons': the Belgian State and Air France.[22]

The Jurisdictional Notice distinguishes between a situation where the state is acting as a public authority in pursuit of public interest and situations where the state acts as a shareholder:

> the prerogatives exercised by a State acting as a public authority rather than as a shareholder, in so far as they are limited to the protection of the public interest, do not constitute control within the meaning of the Merger Regulation to the extent that they have neither the aim nor the effect of enabling the State to exercise a decisive influence over the activity of the undertaking.[23]

The distinction between these two roles that can be played by the state was exemplified in the *Tractebel/Distrigaz (II)* case, where the Belgian State was selling its shares in Distrigaz to Tractebel.[24] The remaining shareholding of the Belgian State would allow it to exercise veto rights over certain strategic decisions of Distrigaz in order to protect public interests in the energy sector. The exercise of such veto rights in the name of public interest

---

(1998) *e-Competitions* July 1998, Art. N° 39373 <www.concurrences.com/en/bulletin/news-issues/july-1998/the-eu-court-of-justice-annuls-for-the-first-time-a-commission-s-decision-under-en> accessed 31 July 2020.

21 Commission Consolidated Jurisdictional Notice under Council Regulation (EC) No 139/2004 on the control of concentrations between undertakings (2008/C 95/01), OJ C95/1, para 12.

22 *Air France/Sabena* (Case IV/M.157) [1992] OJ L272/5, decision of 5 October 1992.

23 Jurisdictional Notice, para 53.

24 *Tractebel/Distrigaz II* (Case IV/M.493) [1994] OJ L249/03, decision of 1 September 1994.

was not regarded as control for the purposes of merger assessment. At the same time, they did not disqualify the Belgian State from being considered a 'person concerned' for the purposes of merger assessment under the EUMR.

1.2 State owned enterprises and the concept of 'single economic unit' under the EU merger control

> *An entity which, owning controlling shareholdings in a company, actually exercises that control by involving itself directly or indirectly in the management thereof must be regarded as taking part in the economic activity carried on by the controlled undertaking.*[25]

The EUMR applies to 'significant structural changes',[26] which are 'bringing about a lasting change in the control of the undertakings concerned and therefore in the structure of the market'.[27] These changes are defined by the concept of 'concentration', which can result from a merger of two or more previously independent undertakings or parts of undertakings or an acquisition, by one or more persons, of direct or indirect control of the whole or parts of one or more other undertakings.[28] The term 'concentration' also applies to the joint venture performing on a lasting basis all the functions of an autonomous economic entity.[29] As a result, concentration is always related to the change of control over an undertaking or part thereof, on a lasting basis. The concept of concentration for the purposes of the merger control only refers to mergers and acquisitions of control between previously independent undertakings. A concentration should be distinguished from an internal restructuring within a group of companies, which may take one of the following forms: (1) increases in shareholdings not accompanied by changes of control; (2) restructuring operations such as a merger of a dual listed company into a single legal entity or a merger of subsidiaries.[30] This creates an exceptional situation when both the acquiring and the target undertakings are owned by the state (its public institutions or local administration such as provinces, states, municipalities, etc.). In such cases, the

---

25 *Ministero dell'Economia e delle Finanze v Cassa di Risparmio di Firenze SpA, Fondazione Cassa di Risparmio di San Miniato and Cassa di Risparmio di San Miniato SpA* (Case C-222/04) [2006] ECR I-00289, judgment of 10 January 2006, para 112.
26 EUMR, recital 8.
27 Ibid., recital 20.
28 Ibid., Article 3(1). See also Jurisdictional Notice, para 7.
29 Ibid., Article 3(4).
30 Jurisdictional Notice, para 51.

determination on whether a specified transaction is a concentration under the EUMR or an internal restructuring will depend on whether prior to the concentration, the undertakings concerned were part of the same economic entity.

If two SOEs 'were formerly part of different economic units having an independent power of decision, the operation will be deemed to constitute a concentration and not an internal restructuring'.[31] For example, 'several SOEs will be considered to be under the same centre of commercial decision-making where they are part of the same holding company owned by the State'.[32] In the *Alcan/Insepal/Palco* merger case, the Commission examined the acquisition of Productos Aluminio de Consumo, S.A. (Palco), which was a subsidiary of Industria Española del Aluminio, S.A. (Insepal), which in turn was a subsidiary of the Spanish State holding INI.[33] The Commission regarded the whole INI Group as a relevant 'single economic unit'.[34]

This presumption, however, can be rebutted by evidence showing that despite being formally controlled by the same state entity, two SOEs are exercising autonomous decision making. For example, in the *Texaco/Norsk Hydro* case, the Commission considered whether two Norwegian SOEs – Norsk Hydro and Statoil – belong to the same economic unit.[35] On the basis of the available evidence, the Commission concluded that 'the commercial activities of these two companies are not coordinated through the intervention of their common shareholder, the Norwegian State'.[36] As a result, Norsk Hydro was regarded as an autonomous economic unit with an independent power of decision.[37]

A similar approach was taken by the Commission in the *Neste/IVO* case concerning a merger of two SOEs, where the Finnish State held 83.17% and 95.6% of the shares, respectively.[38] The Commission established that the Finnish 'state exercises its ownership control only in questions relating to the shareholding of the state, such as sales of shares, listings'.[39] In the absence of

---

31　Ibid., para 52.
32　Kyriakos Fountoukakos and Camille Puech-Baron, 'The EU Merger Regulation and Transactions Involving States or State-Owned Enterprises: Applying Rules Designed for the EU to the People's Republic of China' (2012) *Concurrences* N 1–2012, Art. N° 41904 <www.concurrences.com/en/review/issues/no-1-2012/articles-en/The-EU-merger-regulation-and> accessed 31 July 2020, 48.
33　*Alcan/Insepal/Palco* (Case IV/M.322) [1993] OJ L114/05, decision of 14 April 1993.
34　Ibid., para 13.
35　*Texaco/Norsk Hydro* (Case IV/M.511) [1995] OJ L23/03, decision of 9 January 1995.
36　Ibid., para 26.
37　See *Norsk Hydro/Saga* (Case IV/M.1573) [1999], decision of 5 July 1999.
38　*Neste/IVO* (Case IV/M.931) [1998] OJ L218/04, decision of 2 June 1998.
39　Ibid., para 8.

evidence as to any prior coordination between the two companies, the Commission concluded that they constituted two independent economic entities for the purpose of the merger control. As a result, due to the absence of the common center of control, the two SOEs were regarded as independent market players and their merger was examined as a concentration within the meaning of the EUMR. A similar situation appeared in the *CEA Industrie/ France Telecom/SGS-Thomson* case, where two French SOEs – CEA Industrie and France Telecom – acquired joint control over SGS-Thomson.[40] CEA Industrie was a holding company for the French Atomic Energy Commission, a public research institution of the French government. France Telecom was a state owned public communications provider. For the purpose of exercising the joint control over SGS-Thomson, the two SOEs formed a subsidiary, in which they appointed the board of directors with three appointees of CEA Industrie and two appointees of France Telecom.[41]

In 2008, in the midst of the global financial crisis, the German State has established the Financial Market Stabilization Fund (*Sonderfonds Finanzmarktstabilisierung*, or SoFFin) to serve as an investment vehicle for state intervention in the banking and financial sectors to help financial institutions overcome liquidity squeezes and strengthen their equity basis. SoFFin, which was controlled by the Financial Market Stabilization Agency (*Finanzmarktstabilisierungsanstalt*), notified the acquisition of control over Hypo Real Estate Holding AG, a German financial company engaged in the financing of the commercial real estate.[42] As the target undertaking would not retain an independent power of decision after the concentration, the Commission had to establish which entity, SoFFin, the Financial Market Stabilization Agency, or the German State, should be viewed as the ultimate acquiring entity.[43]

The Commission established that SoFFin's controlling entity, the Financial Market Stabilization Agency, was controlled by the management committee, appointed by the Federal Ministry of Finance in consultation with the German Central Bank.[44] The major decisions of the Financial Market Stabilization Agency had to be approved by the steering committee, which included several representatives of the German federal government. These circumstances showed that both SoFFin and its controlling entity were

---

40 *CEA Industrie/France Telecom/SGS-Thomson* (Case IV/M.216) [1993] OJ L68/05, decision of 22 February 1993.

41 Ibid., para 9.

42 *Soffin/Hypo Real Estate* (Case COMP/M.5508) [2009] OJ L147/8, decision of 14 May 2009.

43 Ibid., para 7.

44 Ibid., para 10.

supervised by the Ministry of Finance, which was authorized to substitute SoFFin and the Agency in the decision making.[45] The Commission concluded that the Ministry of Finance, the federal government, or the German State could constitute an economic unit that has an independent power of decision.[46] There was no final determination made on this issue: 'It can therefore be left open whether the appropriate economic unit with an independent power of decision is at the level of BMF or at a higher level such as the Federal Government or the Bund'.[47]

In Austria, the federal Ministry of Finance sought to acquire control over Hypo Alpe-Adria-Bank International AG and notified this transaction to the Commission to be cleared under the EUMR rules.[48] The Ministry of Finance had already acquired control over Kommunalkredit Austria AG. The federal government also controlled Förderbank Austria, which provided financing to SMEs and regional development. As a result, the Commission was set to establish whether the ministry, the federal government, or the Austrian State should be viewed as the ultimate power of decision for financial institutions it controlled. However, no determination was made in that regard, as it didn't affect the competitive assessment.[49]

In 2009, the French SOE Electricité de France S.A. (EDF) set to acquire the second biggest electricity operator in Belgium, SPE S.A., which was controlled by a holding company Segebel.[50] The French State also had a shareholding in GDF Suez (Electrabel), which raised concerns as to possible coordination between the undertakings concerned.[51] These shareholdings were managed by the Government Shareholding Agency (*Agence des Participations de l'Etat* or APE). Among the relevant factors indicating the possibility of coordinating the commercial operations of the SOEs, the Commission considered: '(1) the existence of interlocking directorships

45 Ibid., para 13.
46 Ibid., para 15.
47 Ibid., para 25.
48 *Republic of Austria/Hypo Group Alpe Adria* (Case COMP/M.5861) [2010] OJ L236/1, decision of 4 August 2010.
49 Ibid., para 9.
50 *EDF/Segebel* (Case COMP/M.5549) [2009] OJ L57/9, decision of 12 November 2009. See John Gatti, 'The EU Commission conditionally Clears a Merger in the Energy Sector (*EDF/Segebel*)' (2009) *e-Competitions* November 2009, Art. N° 37508 <www.concurrences. com/en/bulletin/news-issues/november-2009/the-eu-commission-conditionally-clears-a-merger-in-the-energy-sector-edf-en> accessed 31 July 2020; Krisztian Kecsmar and others, 'The EU Commission Approves, Subject to Remedies, an Acquisition in the Belgian Electricity Market (*EDF / Segebel*)' (2009) *e-Competitions* November 2009, Art. N° 34864 <www.concurrences.com/en/bulletin/news-issues/november-2009/the-eu-commission-approves-subject-to-remedies-acquisition-in-the-belgian-en> accessed 31 July 2020.
51 Ibid., para 89.

between undertakings owned by the same acquiring entity; (2) the existence of adequate safeguards ensuring that commercially sensitive information is not shared between such undertakings'.[52] Without going into the details of the APE's exercise of the shareholding rights of the State, the Commission pointed out that there were no interlocking directorships between the two companies and no other evidence that would suggest that the French State would compromise commercial and business autonomy of these undertakings.[53] This conclusion, based primarily on the previous conduct of EDF and GDF, was criticized by commentators who pointed out that 'wishing to avoid rather political question whether GDF and EDF enjoy autonomy from the State, the Commission instead focused its attention on the independence of both undertakings vis-a-vis each other'.[54]

1.3 State owned enterprises and concentrations of 'Community dimension'

> *The Merger Regulation's Article 1, which applies the Regulation to all concentrations with a Community dimension, can be regarded as a wide definition article that poses little limitation on the Commission's jurisdiction. The wide definition, which relies upon the undertaking's turnover, allows the Commission to assert jurisdiction over transactions, which later may be found to have little or no influence on the common market.[55]*

The EUMR will only apply to the concentrations that have 'Community dimension' based on the following cumulative turnover thresholds: (1) the combined aggregate worldwide turnover of all the undertakings concerned is more than EUR 5,000 million; and (2) the aggregate Community-wide turnover of each of at least two of the undertakings concerned is more than EUR 250 million.[56] Alternatively, the concentration will have a 'Community dimension' where (1) the combined aggregate worldwide turnover of all the undertakings concerned is more than EUR 2,500 million; (2) in each of at least three Member States, the combined aggregate turnover of all the undertakings concerned is more than EUR 100 million; (3) in each of at least three Member States included for the purpose of point (b), the

---

52 Ibid., para 93.
53 Ibid., para 97.
54 Jochem de Kok, 'Chinese SOEs under EU Competition Law' (2017) 40 *World Competition and Economics Review* 583, 591.
55 Ariel Erzachi, 'Limitations on the Extraterritorial Reach of the European Merger Regulation' (2001) 22 *European Competition Law Review* 137, 141.
56 EUMR, Article 1(2).

aggregate turnover of each of at least two of the undertakings concerned is more than EUR 25 million; and (4) the aggregate Community-wide turnover of each of at least two of the undertakings concerned is more than EUR 100 million.[57]

The aforementioned aggregate turnovers are calculated by adding together the respective turnovers of the undertakings directly involved in the concentration (i.e. acquiring and target undertakings) as well as the undertakings that have control over and those controlled by the undertakings involved in the concentration.[58] In relation to SOEs, one should address the following question: 'since the ultimate owners of SOEs are often state governments, should all other SOEs owned by the state government be treated as affiliated and therefore be included in the threshold analysis?'[59] In order to avoid discrimination between SOEs and other companies, the EUMR mandates that

> in the public sector, calculation of the turnover of an undertaking concerned in a concentration needs, therefore, to take account of undertakings making up an economic unit with an independent power of decision, irrespective of the way in which their capital is held or of the rules of administrative supervision applicable to them.[60]

Therefore, in relation to the SOEs, the calculation of turnover does not automatically extend over all SOEs controlled by the same state. It will only take into account those SOEs that constitute an 'economic unit with an independent power of decision'.[61]

In that respect, the Jurisdictional Notice further clarifies that

> where a State-owned company is not subject to any coordination with other State-controlled holdings, it should be treated as independent for the purposes of Article 5, and the turnover of other companies owned by that State should not be taken into account.[62]

In cases where 'several State-owned companies are under the same independent centre of commercial decision-making, then the turnover of those

57 Ibid., Article 1(3).
58 Ibid., Article 5(4).
59 Organisation for Economic Co-Operation and Development, 'Competition Law and State-Owned Enterprises – Contribution from BIAC' (2018) DAF/COMP/GF/WD(2018)73 <https://one.oecd.org/document/DAF/COMP/GF/WD(2018)73/en/pdf> accessed 31 July 2020, 3.
60 EUMR, recital 22; Jurisdictional Notice, para 192.
61 Jurisdictional Notice, para 193.
62 Ibid., para 194.

businesses should be considered part of the group of the undertaking concerned for the purposes of Article 5'.[63] As a result, already at the stage of calculating the aggregate turnover of all undertakings conserved in order to establish the applicability of the EUMR, the EU Commission will have to make a determination in relation to the scope of 'single economic unit' encompassing certain SOEs controlled by the same state.

Because many of the Commission's clearance decisions in merger cases involving SOEs do not contain a detailed assessment on the scope of the respective economic unit, the determinations made about the calculation of the aggregate turnover of the 'undertakings concerned' provide an implied answer on that subject. For example, in 2007, the Commission assessed the acquisition by KazMunaiGaz, a Kazakh SOE, of Rompetrol, a Romanian petroleum company.[64] When calculating the relevant turnover of the acquiring undertaking, the Commission considered only the turnover of KazMunaiGaz without any consideration of other Kazakhstan's SOEs in the energy sector.[65] In another case, the Commission assessed the joint venture established by Rolls Royce and Singapore Airlines, a listed SOE controlled by Singapore through its holding company Temasek Holdings Pte Ltd.[66] The calculation of the aggregate turnover considered only Singapore Airlines and its subsidiaries without accounting for other companies controlled by Singapore through Temasek Holdings.[67] Only when Temasek acted as an acquiring party in a concentration involving the acquisition of control over Swiss company Gategroup, the Commission considered it as a 'single economic unit', which also included Singapore Airlines.[68] A similar approach was taken by the Commission in the cases concerning Qatar Airways, a national flag carrier of the State of Qatar, controlled through the Qatar Holdings, a holding company of the Qatar Investment Authority.[69]

63 Ibid.
64 *Kazmunaigaz/Rompetrol* (Case COMP/M.4934) [2007] OJ L31/2, decision of 19 November 2007. See also *CEFCI/JSC/KazMunaiGaz/Rompetrol France* (Case COMP/M.8319) [2016] OJ C3/2, decision of 23 December 2016.
65 Ibid., para 5.
66 *Singapore Airlines/Rolls-Royce* (Case IV/M.1506) [1999] OJ L176/11, decision of 10 May 1999.
67 Ibid., para 5. See also *Singapore Airlines/Virgin Atlantic* (Case COMP/M.1855) [2000] OJ L110/08, decision of 23 March 2000, para 12.
68 EU Commission press release MEX/19/5499 'Mergers: Commission Clears Acquisition of Gategroup by Temasek and RRJ Capital' (30 August 2019) <https://ec.europa.eu/commission/presscorner/detail/en/MEX_19_5499> accessed 31 July 2020. *Temasek/RRJ Master Fund III/Gategroup* (Case COMP/M.9418) [2019], decision of 29 August 2019.
69 *Qatar Airways/Alisarda/Meridiana* (Case COMP/M.8361) [2017] OJ C122/1, decision of 22 March 2017, para 15.

A more illustrative example of the determination of the economic unit for the purpose of aggregate turnover calculation can be extracted from the economic concentration cases involving Russian SOEs. There have been a number of cases, some of which were decided under the simplified procedure, concerning the Russian state owned energy conglomerate Gazprom.[70] Although Gazprom is an open joint stock company with its shares traded on the Moscow Stock Exchange, it is at the same time 'a major geopolitical tool available to the Russian state which can force other states to submit to Russia's demands in the area of energy'.[71] For the purpose of establishing the 'Community dimension', the Commission has taken into account the turnover of the members of the Gazprom group, without considering other Russian SOEs.[72] Furthermore, the competitive assessment of various foreclosure strategies by Gazprom did not contain any consideration of its state ownership and was based purely on the economic considerations such as recoupment in predatory pricing strategies.[73]

The implied determination that Gazprom could be considered as an economic unit with independent power of decision that is separate from other Russian SOEs was challenged in the *Rosneft/TNK-BP* merger case[74] where the Commission assessed the corporate governance of the Russian SOEs in the oil and gas exploration and production sector.[75] In that case, the Commission was required to determine whether Rosneft and other Russian SOEs in the oil and gas sector, such as Gazprom, Zarubezhneft, and Transneft, would constitute a single economic unit. The Commission has considered that the Russian State participated in the major decision making of Rosneft through the appointments of the SOE's top management: (1) Russian State, through another SOE, Rosneftegaz, held 75.16% of shares in Rosneft,

70 *Gazprom/Sibneft* (Case COMP/M.3999) [2005] OJ L295/20, decision of 18 November 2005; *Dresdner Bank/GazpromBank/JV* (Case COMP/M.4376) [2006] OJ L06/6, decision of 19 December 2006; *Gazprom Schweiz/Promgas* (Case COMP/M.6409) [2011] OJ C361/6, decision of 2 December 2011.

71 P. Sean Morris, 'Iron Curtain at the Border: Gazprom and the Russian Blocking Order to Prevent the Extraterritoriality of EU Competition Law' (2014) 35 *European Competition Law Review* 601, 603.

72 *Gazprom/A2A/JV* (Case COMP/M.5740) [2010] OJ L214/1, decision of 16 June 2010, para 10; *Fortum Corporation/OAO Gazprom/AS Eesti Gas/AS Vorguteenus Valdus* (Case COMP/M.7272) [2014] OJ C272/1, decision of 7 August 2014, para 12.

73 See *Gazprom/Wintershall/Target Companies* (Case COMP/M.6910) [2014] OJ C121/1, decision of 3 December 2013.

74 *Rosneft/TNK-BP* (Case COMP/M.6801) [2013] OJ C107/1, decision of 8 March 2013.

75 See also *Rosneft Oil Company/MP/Ruhr Oil* (Case COMP/M.6147) [2011] OJ L111/9, decision of 10 March 2011; *Rosneft/Morgan Stanley Global Oil Merchanting Unit* (Case COMP/M.7318) [2014] OJ C325/2, decision of 3 September 2014; *GE/Rosneft/JV* (Case COMP/M.8820) [2018] OJ C165/1, decision of 4 April 2018.

which allowed it, as a majority shareholder, to appoint, remove, and set the remuneration of the board of directors; (2) some of the state-appointed members of the Rosneft's board of directors concurrently held directorship positions in other Russian SOEs active in the oil and gas industry; (3) the board of directors approved the long-term strategy of Rosneft as well as the plans for its financial and business operations; (4) the evidence suggested that Rosneft's chief executive officer (CEO) followed the instructions from the Russian top political leadership.[76] On the basis of these factors, the Commission concluded that the Russian State had powers to interfere with the strategic investment decisions of Rosneft.[77]

The apparent discordance between the conclusions reached in *Rosneft/ TNK-BP* and other cases concerning Russian SOEs in the energy sector can be explained in the following way. Although the determination of the 'single economic unit' for the purpose of aggregate turnover calculation is important for applicability of the EU merger control, the determinations made at that stage traditionally considered a more narrow scope of that unit when compared with the substantive assessment of the SOE-related concentrations. For instance, the consideration of the Gazprom's turnover without other Russian SOEs was sufficient for reaching the 'Community dimension'. As a result, the Commission simply avoided a higher evidentiary burden that would be required if the turnovers of all Russian SOEs in the energy field will be added together thus encompassing a broader 'single economic unit'. The Commission's pragmatism was explained in the following way:

> instead of requiring a precise figure for turnover corresponding to the exact boundaries set for the economic unit, the Commission allowed the parties to provide the turnover of just one additional SOE in the economic unit, as this was sufficient to demonstrate that the thresholds were exceeded.[78]

At a later stage, when the Commission had to consider the potential anti-competitive effects of the notified mergers involving Russian SOEs, the Commission resorted to the so-called worst case scenario considering the situation where the Russian SOEs would indeed coordinate their commercial practices acting as members of the 'single economic unit'.

---

76 *Rosneft/TNK-BP*, para 7.
77 Ibid., para 8.
78 Genevieve Lallemand-Kirche, Caroline Tixier and Henri Piffaut, 'The Treatment of State-Owned Enterprises in EU Competition Law: New Developments and Future Challenges' (2017) 8 *Journal of European Competition Law & Practice* 295, 297.

A similar approach was taken by the Commission in the *SFPI/Dexia* case, in which the Belgian State, through its investment company SFPI/FPIM, had acquired control over Dexia.[79] The Commission had

> to assess whether SFPI/FPIM constitutes an economic unit with independent power of decision or whether decisions are made at a higher level than SFPI/FPIM, namely by the Belgian State itself in which case the turnover of other undertakings than those controlled by SFPI/FPIM would need to be added for the purpose of calculating the turnover to be taken into account to establish jurisdiction in this case.[80]

However, since the turnover of SFPI/FPIM and its subsidiaries had already reached the 'Community dimension', no further assessment was deemed necessary.[81]

1.4 State owned enterprises and substantive assessment under the EU Merger Regulation

> *The real test for the Commission's policy vis-à-vis SOEs would come when the Commission would oppose mergers involving foreign SOEs, and in particular when SOEs which would not be parties to the merger would be involved.*[82]

When it comes to the substantive assessment of the notified concentrations involving SOEs, the following issues need to be addressed in order to estimate the likely (anti)competitive effects of such concentrations on the relevant markets. The first issue is related to the forecast of the market conduct of the SOE in question, which may develop into the foreclosure scenarios limiting competition on the relevant market. Such theories of anti-competitive harm should be assessed taking into account the exercise of the state control over the SOE's decision making as well as any other forms of state support that can have an effect on the SOE's capacity and willingness to engage in anti-competitive practices. For example, the 'entrenched market positions or subsidies and public service obligations, may lead to specific anti-competitive conduct like predation by cross-subsidisation from

---

79 *SFPI/Dexia* (Case COMP/M.6812) [2013] OJ C92/4, decision of 21 February 2013.

80 Ibid., para 20.

81 Ibid., para 21.

82 Piet Jan Slot, 'The Application of the EU Merger Control Rules to State Owned Enterprises' (2015) 36 *European Competition Law Review* 484, 491.

subsidised non-commercial activities to commercial ones'.[83] The economic analysis of the foreclosure strategies applied by the SOEs in the US led Sappington and Sidak to conclude that 'SOEs may have strong incentives to engage in anticompetitive activities that serve to expand the scale and scope of their operations'.[84] As a result, the authors suggested to adjust the benchmarks used to evaluate the profitability of various foreclosure scenarios that could be implemented by the SOEs. The Commission acknowledged these findings but found that they will be applicable to purely state owned companies rather than to partly privatized and publicly traded companies.[85] Furthermore, the profitability may not be the primary objective pursued by the SOEs. As noted by Sokol,

> government support for SOEs through government created distortions (e.g., a large reserve sector, implicit loan guarantees, preferences for zoning) allows SOEs to price below its marginal cost due to the explicit and implicit subsidies that governments grant SOEs and not their private competitors.[86]

The second issue that should be considered during the competitive assessment of the SOE-related concentrations is whether possible coordination with other SOEs could be conducive to the implementation of the anticompetitive foreclosure scenarios. The second issue is closely related to the determination of the 'single economic unit' that was discussed earlier in this chapter. However, even if other SOEs have not been included in the relevant 'single economic unit', the common state ownership and exercise of the state control may facilitate anti-competitive behavior post-merger. For example, in the *Rosneft/TNK-BP* case, in its competitive assessment of the notified acquisition, the Commission applied the 'worst case scenario' approach and considered all Russian SOEs active in the oil and gas sector as a single economic entity.[87] For example, when assessing effects on natural gas market, the Commission attributed the activities of Gazprom, one of

---

83 Phil Baumann, 'When State Enterprises Have Deeper Pockets: Ensuring Competitive Neutrality in Cross-Border M&A' in Katia Fach Gómez, Anastasios Gourgourinis and Catharine Titi (eds.) *International Investment Law and Competition Law* (Springer, 2020), 87.
84 David E. M. Sappington and J. Gregory Sidak, 'Competition Law for State-Owned Enterprises' (2003) 71 *Antitrust Law Journal* 479, 522.
85 Organisation for Economic Co-Operation and Development, 'State Owned Enterprises and the Principle of Competitive Neutrality', footnote 2.
86 Daniel Sokol, 'Competition Policy and Comparative Corporate Governance of State-Owned Enterprises' (2009) *Brigham Young University Law Review* 1713, 1775.
87 *Rosneft/TNK-BP*, para 9.

the largest producers and suppliers of natural gas worldwide, to Rosneft.[88] The examination of the merger's effects on supply of crude oil included the consideration of the actions by Transneft, another Russian SOE, which controlled access to the Druzhba pipeline, through which crude oil was transported to landing points in Lithuania, Poland, Germany, the Czech Republic, Slovakia, and Hungary.[89] However, in a subsequent decision involving Rosneft's acquisition of Morgan Stanley's crude oil and petroleum products merchanting activities, the Commission in its competitive assessment did not mention any horizontal overlaps with other Russian SOEs on the market for trading of crude oil and refined petroleum products.[90]

Although the determination of the 'single economic unit' for the purpose of deciding on whether a transaction represents a concentration under the EUMR and calculating the relevant turnovers for checking against the 'Community dimension' thresholds, the Commission is not precluded to take into account possible coordination among the SOEs owned by the same state in its competitive assessment. Although the majority of the concentrations are cleared under the simplified procedure, the short-form decisions provide little insight into the Commission's considerations of the aforementioned issues. For example, throughout the years, the Commission has cleared, under the simplified procedure, more than a dozen concentrations involving the Mubadala Development Company, a sovereign wealth fund owned by the government of Abu Dhabi, United Arab Emirates.[91] In a case concerning a joint venture of Mubadala and Rolls Royce, the newly established entity would be active in the supply of maintenance, repair, and overhaul services for certain aircraft engines.[92] In its competitive assessment, the Commission has considered the commercial activities of the two Mubadala's subsidiaries active in the same sector: ADAT and SR Technics. When it comes to other

---

88 Ibid., para 13.
89 Ibid., para 18.
90 *Rosneft/Morgan Stanley Global Oil Merchanting Unit*, paras 25–31.
91 See *Istithmar/Mubadala/DAE/SR Technics* (Case COMP/M.4393) [2006] OJ L300/26, decision of 9 December 2006; *Dubai/Mubadala/Emal JV* (Case COMP/M.4864) [2007] OJ L234/5, decision of 16 October 2007; *Credit Suisse Group/General Electric/Mubadala Development* (Case COMP/M.4990) [2008] OJ L104/5, decision of 13 February 2008; *Tata/Mubadala/Lochmore/Piaggio* (Case COMP/M.5292) [2008] OJ L255/1, decision of 8 October 2008; *Mubadala/General Electric/JV* (Case COMP/M.5417) [2009] OJ L138/3, decision of 18 June 2009; *Mubadala/UTC* (Case COMP/M.5528) [2009] OJ L196/3, decision of 20 August 2009; *Mubadala/Veolia Eau/Azaliya* (Case COMP/M.5691) [2009] OJ L396/15, decision of 5 December 2009; *Mubadala/UTC/Lockheed Martin/Ammroc* (Case COMP/M.6043) [2010] OJ L03/1, decision of 21 December 2010.
92 *Mubadala/Rolls Royce/JV* (Case COMP/M.5399) [2009] OJ L58/4, decision of 16 February 2009.

SOEs controlled by the Abu Dhabi government, the Commission arrived to a different conclusion. When Mubadala and Sony notified their joint acquisition of EMI Music Publishing, the Commission noted that Sony also had a minority interest in Vevo, which was jointly owned by Sony, Universal Music and Abu Dhabi Media, another SOE under the control of Abu Dhabi emirate.[93] Since the two Emirati SOEs did not have any cross-shareholdings and no interlocking directorships, the Commission has accepted the parties' submission that

> Mubadala is an autonomous economic unit with an independent power of decision and as such there can be no coordination between Mubadala (and its subsidiaries) and Abu Dhabi Media (or any other company owned or controlled by the Government of Abu Dhabi).[94]

In 2016, the Abu Dhabi government decided to merge Mubadala with another SOE under its control – International Petroleum Investment Company. The transaction was notified under Article 3(1) EUMR as a 'merger of two or more previously independent undertakings or parts of undertakings' and the Commission cleared the concentration under a simplified procedure, which does not provide any insights on the assessment of the actual autonomy of the two Emirati SOEs.[95] In 2019, the Commission cleared a merger in the aquaculture sector where Mubadala acted as one of the acquiring undertakings.[96] The case resulted in a conditional clearance with a number of commitments assumed by the merging parties.

The Commission also investigated merger cases involving Qatar Holding, an investment holding company founded by the Qatar Investment Authority, the sovereign investment fund of the State of Qatar. In one of such cases concerning the business travel management services, the Commission considered the likelihood of foreclosure scenarios taking into account the hotel businesses of Qatar Holding as well as the activities of its subsidiary, Qatar Airways.[97] In another case concerning Qatar Holding's investment in the London Heathrow Airport, the Commission considered the former's non-controlling interests in other UK airports as well as its

---

93 *Sony/Mubadala Development/EMI Music Publishing* (Case COMP/M.6459) [2012] OJ C196/1, decision of 19 April 2012.
94 Ibid., footnote 151.
95 *IPIC/Mubadala* (Case COMP/M.8235) [2016] OJ C429/1, decision of 17 November 2016.
96 *Amerra/Mubadala/Nireus/Selonda* (Case COMP/M.9110) [2019] OJ C347/7, decision of 15 February 2019.
97 *American Express Company/Qatar Holding/GBT* (Case COMP/M.7238) [2014] OJ C244/2, decision of 20 June 2014, paras 27–32.

control of Qatar Airways, which together with British Airways participated in the One World Alliance.[98]

1.5 Non-controlling state shareholdings under the EU Merger Regulation

> *The state is not the owner of an enterprise (or the state holds just a minority block of shares, not sufficient to exercise control), yet, through various types of tools, both regulatory and non-regulatory, it de facto controls this enterprise.*[99]

Based on the definition of concentration under the EUMR, the acquisition of minority shareholdings that does not confer the control over the target undertakings will not be subject to notification for merger assessment.[100] Nevertheless, the existence of minority shareholdings are taken into account during the competitive assessment of a concentration, and the Commission's merger assessment practice contains numerous examples when a concentration was cleared subject to divestiture of the certain minority shareholdings.[101] Following the *Ryanair/Aer Lingus* litigation where the General Court held that the Commission had no power to require the divestiture of non-controlling shareholdings when restoring 'the situation prevailing prior to the implementation of the concentration',[102] the Commission has circulated a proposal to fill the alleged enforcement gap and extend the Commission's powers to review the non-controlling shareholdings within the scope of Article 8(4) EUMR.[103] For example, the extension of the concept of 'decisive influence' used for the determination of the concept of 'control' could extend the

---

98 *Ferrovial/Qatar Holding/CDPQ/Baker Street/BAA* (Case COMP/M.6723) [2012], decision of 13 December 2012.

99 Maciej Bałtowski and Piotr Kozarzewski, 'Formal and Real Ownership Structure of the Polish Economy: State-Owned Versus State-Controlled Enterprises' (2016) 28 *Post-Communist Economies* 405, 407.

100 EUMR, Article 3(1).

101 See *Siemens/VA Tech* (Case COMP/M.3653) Commission Decision 2006/899/EC [2005] OJ L353/19; *Glencore/Xstrata* (Case COMP/M.6541) [2014] OJ C109/1, decision of 22 November 2012; *J&J/Actelion* (Case COMP/M.8401) [2017] OJ C281/1, decision of 9 June 2017.

102 Case T-411/07 *Aer Lingus v. Commission* [2010] ECR II-03691, judgment of 6 July 2010, para 66.

103 Commission Staff Working Document 'Towards More Effective EU Merger Control', SWD(2013) 239 final, 25 June 2013.

merger review to non-controlling shareholdings.[104] The opponents of such extension of the EUMR's coverage argued that Article 101 TFEU should be viewed as the appropriate tool to deal with the anti-competitive effects of the non-controlling shareholdings,[105] which may facilitate collusion among undertakings not forming part of a single economic entity.[106] The legislative amendments have not been proposed as 'the Commission is not fully convinced, that the proposed amendments of the current EU merger control regime are "worth" the significant administrative burden on firms'.[107]

Although acquisitions of minority shareholdings without change of control are not subject to notification under the EUMR, their potential anti-competitive effects are continuously examined during the review of the notified concentrations. The Commission's practice involving companies with the minority shareholdings held by a state can be illustrated using the examples of the former SOEs in Poland where the 'reluctant privatization' resulted in 'the preservation of numerous enterprises that are still controlled by the state, although formally the state does not possess any shares in them or has only small packages, which carry insignificant voting rights'.[108] Among such enterprises is integrated petroleum company PKN Orlen. The current (2020) state shareholding in this company is 27.52% held by the State Treasury.[109] At the same time, the articles of association provide that no shareholder can exercise more than 10% of total voting rights at the General Meeting.[110] This restriction, however, does not apply to the State Treasury. This results in a situation where the State Treasury appears as the largest voting rights holder while the voting power of all other shareholders is curbed at a 10% cap. For example, at the General Meeting held on 5 March 2020, the State Treasury exercised 43.01% of voting rights,

---

104 See Catalin Stefan Rusu, 'EU Merger Control and Acquisitions of (Non-Controlling) Minority Shareholdings – the State of Play' (2014) CLaSF Working Paper No 10 <https://clasf.org/working-paper-series/> accessed 31 July 2020, 32.

105 See Kadir Baş, 'Reforming the Treatment of Minority Shareholdings in the EU: Making the Problem Worse Instead of Better?' (2015) 38 *World Competition Law and Economics Review* 77, 98.

106 See Cihan Dogan, 'Acquisitions of Non-Controlling Minority Shareholdings: Assessment from a Competition Policy Perspective' (2016) 17 *Rekabet Dergisi Competition Journal* 4, 26–30.

107 Martin Gassler, 'Non-Controlling Minority Shareholdings and EU Merger Control' (2018) 41 *World Competition Law and Economics Review* 3, 12.

108 Bałtowski and Kozarzewski, 'Formal and Real Ownership Structure of the Polish Economy: State-Owned Versus State-Controlled Enterprises', 409.

109 See PKN Orlen, Shareholders Structure <www.orlen.pl/EN/InvestorRelations/Shareholder ServicesTools/ShareholdersStructure/Pages/default.aspx> accessed 31 July 2020.

110 PKN Orlen, Articles of Association, Article 7(11).

while the total voting rights of all other participating shareholders that had at least 5% of voting rights was 34.97%.[111] These corporate arrangements led the commentators to conclude that the 'Polish state currently controls PKN Orlen via a 27.5% stake'[112] and that the 'Polish state is able to control listed companies even without a majority stake'.[113] As a result, the non-ownership-based means of state control over certain undertakings led to their comparison with the proper SOEs:

> the boards of these companies are subject to politically motivated personnel decisions; the state de facto determines their development strategies, it is also the state that decides every year on the amount of the dividend these companies will pay out.[114]

In 2018, the Polish government decided to consolidate the two biggest petroleum refiners by selling to PKN Orlen a 53% stake in Lotos Group, a Polish SOE.[115] The merger was notified to the EU Commission,[116] which decided to open an in-depth investigation due to concerns that it would lead to an increase in prices of fuel in Poland and other Member States.[117] Following an in-depth investigation of the *PKN Orlen/Lotos Group* merger, the Commission subjected the clearance to a number of structural and behavioral commitments to preserve competition of the motor fuel markets in the Czech Republic and Poland.[118]

111 See PKN Orlen, Shareholders with at least 5% of votes at EGM of PKN ORLEN, Regulatory announcement No. 12 of 5 March 2020 <www.orlen.pl/EN/InvestorRelations/RegulatoryAnnouncements/Pages/Regulatory-announcement-no-12-2020.aspx> accessed 31 July 2020.

112 BNE Intellinews, 'Poland to merge PKN Orlen and Lotos into State Champion' (28 February 2018) <www.intellinews.com/poland-to-merge-pkn-orlen-and-lotos-into-state-champion-137442/> accessed 31 July 2020.

113 Juliette Bretan, 'Political Appointments to Poland's State-Owned Companies See Share Prices Fall' (27 June 2018) <https://emerging-europe.com/news/political-appointments-to-polands-state-owned-companies-see-share-prices-fall/> accessed 31 July 2020.

114 Piotr Kozarzewski and Maciej Bałtowski, 'State Capitalism in Poland' (2019) <www.researchgate.net/publication/332738522_State_Capitalism_in_Poland> accessed 31 July 2020, 26.

115 See James Shotter, 'Polish Government Pushes to Combine Country's Two Biggest Refiners' (28 February 2018) <www.ft.com/content/8607289e-1bdd-11e8-956a-43db76e69936> accessed 31 July 2020.

116 *PKN Orlen/Grupa Lotos* (Case COMP/M.9014) [2020], decision of 14 July 2020.

117 See EU Commission, press release IP/19/5149 'Mergers: Commission Opens in-depth Investigation into PKN Orlen's Proposed Acquisition of Lotos' (7 August 2019) <https://ec.europa.eu/commission/presscorner/detail/en/IP_19_5149> accessed 31 July 2020.

118 EU Commission, press release IP/20/1346 'Mergers: Commission Clears Lotos' Acquisition by PKN Orlen, Subject to Conditions' (14 July 2020) <https://ec.europa.eu/commission/presscorner/detail/en/ip_20_1346> accessed 31 July 2020.

The Commission's assessment of the concentrations involving PKN Orlen dates back to 2005 when it allowed PKN Orlen to acquire 62% shareholding in the Czech SOE Unipetrol.[119] The Commission did not regard the acquiring undertaking as state owned: 'PKN Orlen used to be a state-owned company, which prior to Poland's opening up to an open market economy, was the only company able to produce and sell petroleum products and its derivates'.[120] In that case, PKN Orlen and Lotos Group were regarded as competitors on the markets for gasoline, diesel, and bitumen.[121] In 2012, the Commission cleared PKN Orlen's acquisition of sole control over aviation fuel supplier Petrolot, which was previously under joint control of PKN Orlen and Polish state owned airline LOT.[122] The case was investigated by the Polish national competition authority (NCA) following the Commission's approval of the request for referral under Article 4(4) EUMR. Most recently, the Commission cleared PKN Orlen's acquisition of Energa, a Polish renewable energy operator.[123] Prior to the acquisition, Energa was an SOE controlled by the State Treasury with 52% of the shares (as of 29 November 2019), which accorded the Polish State with a 64% share of voting power at the General Meeting. In its press release, the Commission referred to Energa as 'an energy company active in the generation and wholesale supply, distribution, and retail supply of electricity and other energy-related activities in Poland'.[124] The Commission's merger assessment in the cases involving PKN Orlen indicates that the non-controlling shareholding of the Polish State does not create a presumption of coordinating market conduct of state-invested or state-controlled entities. This approach follows the one adopted by the Polish NCA (UOKiK)[125] assessing SOE-related mergers under the national merger control regime. In 2011, the UOKiK prohibited the acquisition of Energa by PGE, the two SOEs active in generation, trading, and distribution of electricity.[126] Although controlled by the same state, the two companies were viewed as competitors on the electricity markets and their merger would eliminate

---

119 *PKN Orlen/Unipetrol* (Case COMP/M.3543) [2005] OJ L129/02, decision of 20 April 2005.
120 Ibid., para 7.
121 Ibid., paras 34, 50.
122 *PKN Orlen/Petrolot* (Case COMP/M.6683) [2012], decision of 5 September 2012.
123 *PKN Orlen/Energa* (Case COMP/M.9626) [2020] OJ C132/2, decision of 31 March 2020.
124 EU Commission, press release MEX/20/573 'Mergers: Commission Clears Acquisition of Energa by PKN Orlen' (1 April 2020) <https://ec.europa.eu/commission/presscorner/detail/en/MEX_20_573> accessed 31 July 2020.
125 Office of Competition and Consumer Protection (*Urząd Ochrony Konkurencji i Konsumentów*).
126 UOKiK, Decision DKK 1/2011 of 13 January 2011.

competitive pressure and lead to price increases.[127] The UOKiK's prohibition decision has allegedly led to the dismissal of its president for preventing the state-led consolidation of the energy sector.[128] The acquisition of EDF Polska by PGE in 2017 was cleared by the UOKiK after accepting behavioral commitments.[129] The UOKiK was subsequently accused of favoritism in relation to SOEs as the Polish NCA permitted a concentration leading to elimination of the fourth-largest and the only competitor, which was not owned by the Polish State.[130]

Bibliography

Bałtowski M, P Kozarzewski, 'Formal and Real Ownership Structure of the Polish Economy: State-Owned Versus State-Controlled Enterprises' (2016) 28 *Post-Communist Economies* 405.

Baş K, 'Reforming the Treatment of Minority Shareholdings in the EU: Making the Problem Worse Instead of Better?' (2015) 38 *World Competition Law and Economics Review* 77.

Baumann P, 'When State Enterprises Have Deeper Pockets: Ensuring Competitive Neutrality in Cross-Border M&A' in KF Gómez, A Gourgourinis, C Titi (eds.) *International Investment Law and Competition Law* (Springer, 2020).

Bernatt M, 'Illiberal Populism: Competition Law at Risk?' (SSRN, 24 January 2019) <www.ssrn.com/abstract=3321719> accessed 31 July 2020.

De Kok J, 'Chinese SOEs under EU Competition Law' (2017) 40 *World Competition and Economics Review* 583.

Dogan C, 'Acquisitions of Non-Controlling Minority Shareholdings: Assessment from A Competition Policy Perspective' (2016) 17 *Rekabet Dergisi Competition Journal* 4.

---

127 See Robert Gago and Ewa Tabor, 'The Polish Competition Authority Prohibits a Merger in the Energy Sector (*PGE / Energa*)' (2011) *e-Competitions* January 2011, Art. N° 34262 <www.concurrences.com/en/bulletin/news-issues/january-2011/the-polish-competition-authority-prohibits-a-merger-in-the-energy-sector-pge-en> accessed 31 July 2020; Jaroslaw Sroczynski, 'The Polish Competition Court Upholds the Prohibition of a Merger in the Energy Sector, Confirms that Conditions Can Be Granted Also by the Court, Defines when the "Rule of Reason" Can Be Applicable and Consequently Confirms a Non-Primary Meaning of Procedural Omissions of the Competition Authority (PGE)' (2012) *e-Competitions* May 2012, Art. N° 57363 <www.concurrences.com/en/bulletin/news-issues/may-2012/the-polish-competition-court-upholds-the-prohibition-of-a-merger-in-the-energy-en> accessed 31 July 2020.

128 See Marek Martyniszyn and Maciej Bernatt, 'Implementing a Competition Law System: Three Decades of Polish Experience' (2020) 8 *Journal of Antitrust Enforcement* 165, 176–177.

129 UOKiK, Decision DKK-156/2017 of 4 October 2017.

130 See Maciej Bernatt, 'Illiberal Populism: Competition Law at Risk?' (SSRN, 24 January 2019) <https://ssrn.com/abstract=3321719> accessed 31 July 2020, 42–46.

Erzachi A, 'Limitations on the Extraterritorial Reach of the European Merger Regulation' (2001) 22 *European Competition Law Review* 137.

Fountoukakos K, C Puech-Baron, 'The EU Merger Regulation and Transactions Involving States or State-Owned Enterprises: Applying Rules Designed for the EU to the People's Republic of China' (2012) *Concurrences N° 1–2012*, Art. N° 41904 <www.concurrences.com/en/review/issues/no-1-2012/articles-en/The-EU-merger-regulation-and> accessed 31 July 2020.

Gago R, E Tabor, 'The Polish Competition Authority Prohibits a Merger in the Energy Sector (PGE/Energa)' (2011) *e-Competitions* January 2011, Art. N° 34262 <www.concurrences.com/en/bulletin/news-issues/january-2011/the-polish-com petition-authority-prohibits-a-merger-in-the-energy-sector-pge-en> accessed 31 July 2020.

Gassler M, 'Non-Controlling Minority Shareholdings and EU Merger Control' (2018) 41 *World Competition Law and Economics Review* 3.

Gatti J, 'The EU Commission Conditionally Clears a Merger in the Energy Sector (EDF/Segebel)' (2009) *e-Competitions* November 2009, Art. N° 37508 <www.concurrences.com/en/bulletin/news-issues/november-2009/the-eu-commission-conditionally-clears-a-merger-in-the-energy-sector-edf-en> accessed 31 July 2020.

Hacker N, 'The EU Court of Justice Annuls for the First Time a Commission's Decision under the Merger Regulation (Kali+Salz/MDK/Deutsche Treuhand)' (1998) *e-Competitions* July 1998, Art. N° 39373 <www.concurrences.com/en/bulletin/news-issues/july-1998/the-eu-court-of-justice-annuls-for-the-first-time-a-commission-s-decision-under-en> accessed 31 July 2020.

Jones A, 'The Boundaries of an Undertaking in EU Competition Law' (2012) 8 *European Competition Journal* 301.

Kecsmar K, others, 'The EU Commission Approves, Subject to Remedies, an Acquisition in the Belgian Electricity Market (EDF/Segebel)' (2009) *e-Competitions* November 2009, Art. N° 34864 <www.concurrences.com/en/bulletin/news-issues/november-2009/the-eu-commission-approves-subject-to-remedies-acquisition-in-the-belgian-en> accessed 31 July 2020.

Kerstling C, 'Liability of Sister Companies and Subsidiaries in European Competition Law' (2020) 41 *European Competition Law Review* 125.

Lallemand-Kirche G, C Tixier, H Piffaut, 'The Treatment of State-Owned Enterprises in EU Competition Law: New Developments and Future Challenges' (2017) 8 *Journal of European Competition Law & Practice* 295.

Liberatore F, 'Slovak Telekom/Deutsche Telekom AG: the Interplay between EU Competition Law and Sector-Specific Rules in the Electronic Communications Sector' (2019) 40 *European Competition Law Review* 502.

Martyniszyn M, M Bernatt, 'Implementing a Competition Law System: Three Decades of Polish Experience' (2020) 8 *Journal of Antitrust Enforcement* 165.

Morris PS, 'Iron Curtain at the Border: Gazprom and the Russian Blocking Order to Prevent the Extraterritoriality of EU Competition Law' (2014) 35 *European Competition Law Review* 601.

Nowag J, 'SELEX Sistemi Integrati SpA v Commission of the European Communities (C-113/07 P) [2009] E.C.R. I-2207: Redefining the Boundaries between

Undertaking and the Exercise of Public Authority' (2010) 31 *European Competition Law Review* 483.

Organisation for Economic Co-Operation and Development, 'Competition Law and State-Owned Enterprises: Contribution from BIAC' (2018) DAF/COMP/GF/WD (2018)73 <https://one.oecd.org/document/DAF/COMP/GF/WD(2018)73/en/pdf> accessed 31 July 2020.

————, 'Governments as Competitors in the Global Marketplace: Options for Ensuring a Level Playing Field' (2016) <http://e15initiative.org/publications/governments-as-competitors-in-the-global-marketplace-options-for-ensuring-a-level-playing-field/> accessed 31 July 2020.

————, 'Ownership and Governance of State-Owned Enterprises: A Compendium of National Practices' (2018) <www.oecd.org/corporate/Ownership-and-Governance-of-State-Owned-Enterprises-A-Compendium-of-National-Practices.pdf> accessed 31 July 2020.

————, 'State Owned Enterprises and the Principle of Competitive Neutrality' (2009) DAF/COMP(2009)37 <www.oecd.org/daf/competition/46734249.pdf> accessed 31 July 2020.

Rusu CS, 'EU Merger Control and Acquisitions of (Non-Controlling) Minority Shareholdings: The State of Play' (2014) *CLaSF Working Paper No. 10* <https://clasf.org/working-paper-series/> accessed 31 July 2020.

Sappington DEM, JG Sidak, 'Competition Law for State-Owned Enterprises' (2003) 71 *Antitrust Law Journal* 479.

Sinclair D, '"Undertakings" in Competition Law at the Public-Private Interface: An Unhealthy Situation' (2014) 35 *European Competition Law Review* 161.

Slot PJ, 'The Application of the EU Merger Control Rules to State Owned Enterprises' (2015) 36 *European Competition Law Review* 484.

Sokol D, 'Competition Policy and Comparative Corporate Governance of State-Owned Enterprises' (2009) *Brigham Young University Law Review* 1713.

Sroczynski J, 'The Polish Competition Court Upholds the Prohibition of a Merger in the Energy Sector, Confirms That Conditions Can Be Granted Also by the Court, Defines When the "Rule of Reason" Can Be Applicable and Consequently Confirms a Non-Primary Meaning of Procedural Omissions of the Competition Authority (PGE)' (2012) *e-Competitions* May 2012, Art. N° 57363 <www.concurrences.com/en/bulletin/news-issues/may-2012/the-polish-competition-court-upholds-the-prohibition-of-a-merger-in-the-energy-en> accessed 31 July 2020.

Svetlicinii A, 'Back to the Basics: Concepts of Undertaking and Economic Activity in the SELEX Judgment' (2009) 12 *European Law Reporter* 422.

————, 'The Competition Authority of Bosnia & Herzegovina follows EU Competition Law Standards and Rejects an Anticompetitive Agreement Complaint in Relation to Affiliated Companies Being Part of a "Single Economic Entity" (Elektrokontakt/Elektroprivreda/Eldis-tehnika)' (2011) *e-Competitions* February 2011, Art. N° 36981 <www.concurrences.com/en/bulletin/news-issues/february-2011/the-competition-authority-of-bosnia-herzegovina-follows-eu-competition-law-en> accessed 31 July 2020.

————, 'The Court of Bosnia and Herzegovina Quashes the No-Infringement Decision of the Competition Authority Based on the Concept of "Single Economic

Entity" (Elektrokontakt)' (2014) *e-Competitions* January 2014, Art. N° 64923 <www.concurrences.com/en/bulletin/news-issues/january-2014/the-court-of-bosnia-and-herzegovina-quashes-the-no-infringement-decision-of-the-en> accessed 31 July 2020.
————, 'Who Is to Blame? Liability of "Economic Units" for Infringement of EU Competition Law' (2011) 2 *European Law Reporter* 52.
Szydło M, 'Leeway of Member States in Shaping the Notion of an "Undertaking" in Competition Law' (2010) 33 *World Competition Law and Economics Review* 549.

Court of Justice of the European Union

Aer Lingus v Commission (Case T-411/07) [2010] ECR II-03691.
Ambulanz Glockner v Landkreis Südwestpfalz (Case C-475/99) [2001] ECR I-08089.
Commission v France (Case C-159/94) [1997] ECR I-05815.
Commission v Italy (Case C-118/85) [1987] ECR 02599.
Commission v Italy (Case C-158/94) [1997] ECR I-05789.
Commission v Netherlands (Case C-157/94) [1997] ECR I-05699.
Deutsche Telekom AG v Commission (Case T-827/14) [2018] ECR.
Höfner and Elser v Macrotron GmbH (Case C-41/90) [1991] ECR I-01979.
Metsä-Serla Oyj, UPM-Kymmene Oyj, Tamrock Oy and Kyro Oyj Abp v Commission (Case C-294/98 P) [2000] ECR I-10065.
Ministero dell'Economia e delle Finanze v Cassa di Risparmio di Firenze SpA, Fondazione Cassa di Risparmio di San Miniato and Cassa di Risparmio di San Miniato SpA (Case C-222/04) [2006] ECR I-00289.
SELEX Sistemi Integrati SpA v Commission (Case C-113/07 P) [2009] ECR I-02207.
Viho Europe BV v Commission (Case C-73/95 P) [1996] ECR I-05457.

European Commission (merger cases)

Air France/Sabena (Case IV/M.157) [1992] OJ L272/5.
Alcan/Insepal/Palco (Case IV/M.322) [1993] OJ L114/05.
American Express Company/Qatar Holding/GBT (Case COMP/M.7238) [2014] OJ C244/2.
Amerra/Mubadala/Nireus/Selonda (Case COMP/M.9110) [2019] OJ C347/7.
CEA Industrie/France Telecom/SGS-Thomson (Case IV/M.216) [1993] OJ L68/05.
CEFCI/JSC/KazMunaiGaz/Rompetrol France (Case COMP/M.8319) [2016] OJ C3/2.
Credit Suisse Group/General Electric/Mubadala Development (Case COMP/M.4990) [2008] OJ L104/5.
Dresdner Bank/GazpromBank/JV (Case COMP/M.4376) [2006] OJ L06/6.
Dubal/Mubadala/Emal JV (Case COMP/M.4864) [2007] OJ L234/5.
EDF/Segebel (Case COMP/M.5549) [2009] OJ L57/9.
Ferrovial/Qatar Holding/CDPQ/Baker Street/BAA (Case COMP/M.6723) [2012].
Fortum Corporation/OAO Gazprom/AS Eesti Gas/AS Vorguteenus Valdus (Case COMP/M.7272) [2014] OJ C272/1.

Gaz de France/Ruhrgas/Slovensky (Case COMP/M.2791) [2002] OJ L154/08.

Gazprom/A2A/JV (Case COMP/M.5740) [2010] OJ L214/1.

Gazprom Schweiz/Promgas (Case COMP/M.6409) [2011] OJ C361/6.

Gazprom/Sibneft (Case COMP/M.3999) [2005] OJ L295/20.

Gazprom/Wintershall/Target Companies (Case COMP/M.6910) [2014] OJ C121/1.

GE/Rosneft/JV (Case COMP/M.8820) [2018] OJ C165/1.

Glencore/Xstrata (Case COMP/M.6541) [2014] OJ C109/1.

IPIC/Mubadala (Case COMP/M.8235) [2016] OJ C429/1.

Istithmar/Mubadala/DAE/SR Technics (Case COMP/M.4393) [2006] OJ L300/26.

J&J/Actelion (Case COMP/M.8401) [2017] OJ C281/1.

Kali-Salz/MdK/Treuhand (Case IV/M.308) Commission Decision 94/449/EC [1993] OJ L184/38.

Kazmunaigaz/Rompetrol (Case COMP/M.4934) [2007] OJ L31/2.

Mubadala/General Electric/JV (Case COMP/M.5417) [2009] OJ L138/3.

Mubadala/Rolls Royce/JV (Case COMP/M.5399) [2009] OJ L58/4.

Mubadala/UTC (Case COMP/M.5528) [2009] OJ L196/3.

Mubadala/UTC/Lockheed Martin/Ammroc (Case COMP/M.6043) [2010] OJ L03/1.

Mubadala/Veolia Eau/Azaliya (Case COMP/M.5691) [2009] OJ L396/15.

Neste/IVO (Case IV/M.931) [1998] OJ L218/04.

Norsk Hydro/Saga (Case IV/M.1573) [1999].

PKN Orlen/Energa (Case COMP/M.9626) [2020] OJ C132/2.

PKN Orlen/Grupa Lotos (Case COMP/M.9014) [2020].

PKN Orlen/Petrolot (Case COMP/M.6683) [2012].

PKN Orlen/Unipetrol (Case COMP/M.3543) [2005] OJ L129/02.

Qatar Airways/Alisarda/Meridiana (Case COMP/M.8361) [2017] OJ C122/1.

Republic of Austria/Hypo Group Alpe Adria (Case COMP/M.5861) [2010] OJ L236/1.

Rosneft/Morgan Stanley Global Oil Merchanting Unit (Case COMP/M.7318) [2014] OJ C325/2.

Rosneft Oil Company/MP/Ruhr Oil (Case COMP/M.6147) [2011] OJ L111/9.

Rosneft/TNK-BP (Case COMP/M.6801) [2013] OJ C107/1.

SFPI/Dexia (Case COMP/M.6812) [2013] OJ C92/4.

Siemens/VA Tech (Case COMP/M.3653) Commission Decision 2006/899/EC [2005] OJ L353/19.

Singapore Airlines/Rolls-Royce (Case IV/M.1506) [1999] OJ L176/11.

Singapore Airlines/Virgin Atlantic (Case COMP/M.1855) [2000] OJ L110/08.

Soffin/Hypo Real Estate (Case COMP/M.5508) [2009] OJ L147/8.

Sony/Mubadala Development/EMI Music Publishing (Case COMP/M.6459) [2012] OJ C196/1.

Tata/Mubadala/Lochmore/Piaggio (Case COMP/M.5292) [2008] OJ L255/1.

Temasek/RRJ Master Fund III/Gategroup (Case COMP/M.9418) [2019].

Texaco/Norsk Hydro (Case IV/M.511) [1995] OJ L23/03.

Tractebel/Distrigaz II (Case IV/M.493) [1994] OJ L249/03.

2 China's state owned enterprises

Governance and regulation

2.1 State owned enterprises as a pillar of 'socialism with Chinese characteristics'

The fundamental task for our country is to concentrate on achieving socialist modernization along the road of socialism with Chinese characteristics.[1]

The uncontested dominance of the SOEs in the national economy of the People's Republic of China (PRC) is stipulated in various legislative and policy documents. The Constitution of the PRC proclaims that the 'basis of the socialist economic system of the People's Republic of China is socialist public ownership of the means of production, namely, ownership by the whole people and collective ownership by the working people'.[2] Likewise, the Constitution of the Communist Party of China (CPC) proclaims public/ state ownership as a basis of the economic system: 'the Party must uphold and improve the basic economic system whereby public ownership plays a dominant role and economic entities under diverse forms of ownership develop side by side'.[3] The reasons for the existential role the SOEs play for the PRC can be summarized as follows: (1) the very claim that PRC is a socialist country rests on the existence of the SOEs as enterprises owned by the whole people; (2) the SOEs and the assets they control provide an economic and financial basis for the CPC rule; (3) the SOEs have major responsibilities in implementing the economic and industrial policies; (4) the SOEs ensure national security and people's livelihood.[4] Or, as succinctly summed up by Wang,

---

1 Constitution of the People's Republic of China, adopted at the 5th Session of the 5th National People's Congress on 4 December 1982, preamble.
2 Constitution of the People's Republic of China, Article 6.
3 Constitution of the Communist Party of China, revised and adopted at the 19th National Congress of the Communist Party of China on 24 October 2017.
4 See Xin Li and Kjeld Erik Brodsgaard, 'SOE Reform in China: Past, Present and Future' (2013) 31 *Copenhagen Journal of Asian Studies* 54, 64–65.

> SOEs provide the economic foundation for the [CPC]'s reign as they not only enable the Party-state to pay for the requisite human and political expenses, but also cause the citizens of China to depend on the Party-state for a living.[5]

The backbone role of the SOEs in the Chinese economy and society remained largely uncontested even though these enterprises have been undergoing a continuous process of organizational reform. In order to increase the efficiency of the SOEs, the Chinese State has experimented with various forms of organizational structures and operational autonomy. During 1978–1994 the SOEs received limited operational autonomy and possibility to further their own economic interests. In 1984–1992 the contracting system was introduced to increase the managerial autonomy and encourage productivity growth. The reform proponents in the 1990s called for removal of the policy burden from the SOEs, hardening of their budget constraints, and providing them with a level playing field.[6] In 1992, the 14th CPC Central Committee adopted the Decision on the Establishment of the Socialist Market Economy with the aim

> to further transform the management mechanism of state-owned enterprises, and to establish a modern enterprise system which meets the requirements of the market economy and in which the property rights as well as the rights and responsibilities of enterprises are clearly defined, government administration and enterprise management are separated and scientific management is established.[7]

The purpose of this transformation was to make the SOEs take 'responsibility for their own management decisions, profits and losses, and operating risks'.[8] In 1993, with the adoption of the Company Law,[9] the Chinese SOEs obtained a form of a modern enterprise with an ownership-based control system and corporate bodies with distinct responsibilities.[10] It has replaced

5 Jiangyu Wang, 'The Political Logic of Corporate Governance in China's State-Owned Enterprises' (2014) 47 *Cornell International Law Journal* 631, 639.

6 See Justin Yifu Lin, Fang Cai and Zhou Li, 'Competition, Policy Burdens, and State-Owned Enterprise Reform' (1998) 88 *AEA Papers and Proceedings* 422, 426.

7 Decision of the CPC Central Committee on Some Issues Concerning the Establishment of a Socialist Market Economic Structure, 22 November 1993, para 2.

8 Peiyan Zeng, 'The Establishment of the Socialist Market Economy' (2012) 4(3) *Qiushi Journal* <http://english.qstheory.cn/magazine/201203/201210/t20121008_185077.htm> accessed 31 July 2020.

9 Company Law of the People's Republic of China, 29 December 1993.

10 See Kaifeng Yang, 'State-Owned Enterprise Reform in Post-Mao China' (2007) 31 *International Journal of Public Administration* 24, 26–29.

'three old committees', meaning a CPC committee, an employee committee, and a trade union, with 'three new committees' – a board of directors, a board of supervisors, and a shareholder general assembly.[11]

What followed can be labeled as a period of 'privatisation, corporatisation and modernization'[12] during 1993–2002, which encompassed the privatization of numerous small SOEs and consolidation of the remaining larger SOEs into the diversified and integrated industrial SOE groups. The year 2003 was marked by the establishment of the State-Owned Assets Supervision and Administration Commission (SASAC), an institution entrusted to exercise ownership-based state control over the SOEs.[13] The SASAC participated in further consolidation of the state owned sector overseeing SOE-to-SOE mergers. The policy of creating state owned national champions 'let go of the small and hold on to the big' pursued the objective 'to create truly global Chinese companies that could compete with the large multinational companies that dominated global production chains'.[14]

The current phase of reform commenced in 2013, when the 18th CPC Central Committee issued Decision of Several Major Issues of Comprehensively Deepening the Reform.[15] It envisaged strengthening the 'modern enterprise system' by establishing state asset management companies as an additional corporate layer between the SASAC and the SOEs and promotion of the mixed ownership whereby SOEs would welcome private shareholders. The 2015 Guiding Opinions of the State Council pledged 'to promote SOEs to become independent market players in the true sense where they engage in autonomous operations, make profits and assume losses independently, bear risks on their own, practice self-discipline and pursue self-development pursuant to the law'.[16] The SOEs have been divided into two categories based on their primary function: commercial SOEs and public welfare SOEs. The commercial SOEs should fulfil the following functions: (1) enhancing the vitality of the state owned economic sector: (2) amplifying the functions of state owned capital; (3) preserving and increasing

---

11 See Zhaofeng Wang, 'Corporate Governance Under State Control: The Chinese Experience' (2012) 13 *Theoretical Inquiries in Law* 487, 490.

12 Weihuan Zhou, Henry Gao and Xue Bai, 'Building a Market Economy Through WTO-Inspired Reform of State-Owned Enterprises in China' (2019) 68 *International and Comparative Law Quarterly* 977, 980.

13 Interim Regulation on the Supervision and Administration of State-Owned Assets of Enterprises, 27 May 2003.

14 Kjeld Erik Brodsgaard, 'Politics and Business Group Formation in China: The Party in Control?' (2012) 211 *China Quarterly* 624, 628.

15 CPC Central Committee, Decision of Several Major Issues of Comprehensively Deepening the Reform, 12 November 2013.

16 Guiding Opinions of the CPC Central Committee and the State Council on Deepening the Reform of State-Owned Enterprises, 24 August 2015, para 2.

the value of state owned assets.[17] At the same time, the Guiding Opinions specify that there will be certain commercial SOEs 'whose core business belongs to major industries and key fields concerning national security or national economic lifeline'.[18] The Opinions continue:

> the assessment of such SOEs shall not only cover their business performance indicators and the preservation and appreciation of the value of their State-owned assets, but also focus on aspects such as their efforts to serve national strategies, safeguard national security and the operation of the national economy, develop cutting-edge strategic industries and complete special tasks.[19]

The assessment of the public welfare SOEs:

> shall focus on cost control, product and service quality, operating efficiency and support capabilities, while their business performance indicators and the preservation and appreciation of the value of their State-owned assets shall be assessed in a differentiated manner according to different characteristics of such enterprises.[20]

The state asset management companies referred to as 'state-owned capital investment and operating companies' are expected to 'perform shareholder responsibilities with regard to invested enterprises, and effectively assume the responsibilities for preserving and increasing the value of State-owned assets'.[21]

The envisaged operational autonomy of commercial SOEs and their legal separation from the government does not exclude the exercise of the state control and influence over the major decisions. The analysts favoring the OECD recommendations on SOE governance called the Chinese policy makers to 'reduce governmental interference into SOEs' decision making processes; eliminate financial and regulatory benefits conferred on SOEs and upgrade corporate governance standards in SOEs in order to entrench their commercial orientation'.[22] This process, however, was accompanied by the incorporation of the effective control mechanisms that would ensure

---

17 See 2015 Guiding Opinions, para 5.
18 Ibid.
19 Ibid.
20 Ibid., para 6.
21 Ibid., para 13.
22 Ming Du, 'When China's National Champions Go Global: Nothing to Fear but Fear Itself?' (2014) 48 *Journal of World Trade* 1127, 1161.

that the SOEs follow the industrial policies and other objectives of China's economic statecraft. For instance, the Guiding Opinions direct the SOEs to

> optimize the key investment directions and fields for State-owned capital by closely centering around the missions of serving national strategies, and enforcing State industrial policies and the general requirements of adjusting the layout of key industries, and push State-owned capital to gravitate towards important sectors and key fields concerning national security, national economic lifeline and people's livelihood, key infrastructure, forward-looking strategic industries and enterprises with core competitive edges.[23]

As explained by Che, by changing its role from an administrator to an investor the Chinese State has enhanced its capacity to influence the operations of the SOEs as 'the state is able to ensure that SOEs operate in line with the goal of economic development through a non-administrative way that does not undermine market conditions'.[24] In 2013, with the unveiling of the Belt and Road Initiative,[25] the Chinese SOEs have become primary actors involved in foreign investment projects, benefiting from the preferential access to the financing provided by the state owned banks.[26] The SOEs also play a critical role in the Chinese industrial policy Made in China 2025 by developing the strategic industries and high-tech equipment manufacturing, where in the key industry sectors the SOEs' revenue share was estimated at 83% in 2019.[27]

The progress of the SOE reform and the implementation of the sector-specific industrial policies have led to the concentration of certain economic sectors under the dominance of the SOEs, while leaving others more open to competition from private and foreign-owned companies. For example,

23 2015 Guiding Opinions, para 14.
24 Luyao Che, 'Legal Implications of the Deepened Reform of Chinese State-Owned Enterprises: What Can Be Expected from Recent Reforms?' (2016) 8 *Tsinghua China Law Review* 171, 180.
25 State Council, 'Full Text: Action Plan on the Belt and Road Initiative' (30 March 2015), <http://english.www.gov.cn/archive/publications/2015/03/30/content_281475080249035.htm> accessed 31 July 2020.
26 See Vivienne Bath, 'Chinese Companies and Outbound Investment: The Balance between Domestic and International Concerns' in Lisa Toohey, Colin B. Picker and Jonathan Greenacre (eds.) *China in the International Economic Order: New Directions and Changing Paradigms* (Cambridge 2015).
27 Max J. Zenglein and Anna Holzmann, 'Evolving Made in China 2025: China's Industrial Policy in the Quest for Global Teach Leadership' (Mercator Institute for China Studies 2019) <https://merics.org/en/report/evolving-made-china-2025> accessed 31 July 2020, 45.

Pearson presented the Chinese economy as a three-tiered structure with each tier representing a different degree of state control and intervention into various economic sectors.[28] Thus, the top tier includes strategic industries (heavy industries, grain supply, finance, energy, petroleum, aviation, telecommunications, construction, banking, insurance) that see the majority of the centrally owned SOEs.[29] These Chinese 'national champions' are controlled by the Central SASAC and are subject to the industrial policies set by the National Development and Reform Commission (NDRC) and other sector-specific regulators. Most of these sectors are also heavily regulated, which explains the presence of sector-specific regulators. The middle tier covers the sectors that are considered important but require less centralized oversight (automobiles, pharmaceuticals, chemicals, steel, telecommunications equipment, heavy industrial machinery, biotechnology, alternative energy manufacturing). These sectors see a more diverse landscape of ownership, including provincial and municipal SOEs controlled by the local governments as well as large private firms.[30] Finally, the third tier includes medium and small manufacturing, personal services, and retail.[31] These economic sectors see a large number of privately owned small and medium enterprises. The third tier industries are covered by a regulatory and administrative oversight of a wide range of ministries and specialized state agencies, such as the Ministry of Commerce (MOFCOM), the State Administration for Market Regulation (SAMR), the State Administration for Industry of Commerce, etc. A special role in the oversight of the private enterprises should be attributed to the grassroots organizations of the CPC, which are often embraced by the business owners as a channel for political representation of the entrepreneurial interests.[32]

Since the present work does not aim at providing a comprehensive overview of the Chinese SOE system, the following sections will be focused on the two institutional channels through which the Chinese State can exercise control over its SOEs: (1) ownership-based control through the SASAC as a state shareholder and (2) political control through CPC organs. The analysis of these two channels of control will inform the discussion on Chinese SOE governance analyzed by the Commission under the EUMR, as discussed in Chapter 3.

---

28 Margaret M. Pearson, 'State-Owned Business and Party-State Regulation in China's Modern Political Economy' in Barry Naughton and Kellee S. Tsai (eds.) *State Capitalism, Institutional Adaptation, and the Chinese Miracle* (Cambridge 2015), 27–45.

29 Ibid., 32.

30 Ibid., 34.

31 Ibid., 35.

32 Heike Holbig, 'The Party and Private Entrepreneurs in the PRC' (2002) 16 *Copenhagen Journal of Asian Studies* 30, 53.

2.2 Ownership-based control: the State-Owned Assets Supervision and Administration Commission

> *Known as the State-owned Assets Supervision and Administration Commission of the State Council, 'SASAC' is the world's largest controlling shareholder. SASAC is undoubtedly one of the most powerful economic actors in the world today. Yet few people outside of China understand its critical role.*[33]

The adoption of the Company Law in 1993 laid the legal ground for the establishment of the 'modern state ownership' system, which freed the SOEs from the policy burden of providing public goods for their workers and the public at large and placed them under the state control through the appointment of the managers and their responsibility toward the majority shareholder – the Chinese State.[34] The Company Law referred to SOE as the 'wholly state-owned company' defined as

> limited liability company invested wholly by the state, for which the State Council or the local people's government authorizes the state-owned assets supervision and administration institution of the people's government at the same level to perform the functions of the capital contributor.[35]

The SASAC as the State Council's 'ownership agency' was set up in 2003 and given the powers to exercise ownership rights in 196 companies, often regarded as centrally owned or centrally controlled SOEs.[36] The Interim Regulations define the SASAC as 'the ad hoc body directly affiliated to the State Council that, on behalf of the State Council, performs the contributor's duties and is responsible for the supervision and administration of the state-owned assets in enterprises'.[37] The main duties of the SASAC are formulated broadly: (1) performing the contributor's duties and protecting the owner's rights and interests; (2) directing and promoting the reform and

---

33 Mark Wu, 'The China, Inc. Challenge to Global Trade Governance' (2016) 57 *Harvard International Law Journal* 261, 271.
34 See Rui Guo, 'The Creation of Modern State Ownership: Legal Transplantation and the Rise of Modern State-Owned Big Businesses in China' (2013) 4 *Peking University Journal of Legal Studies* 69, 78–84.
35 Company Law, Article 64.
36 See Barry Naughton, 'The Transformation of the State Sector: SASAC, the Market Economy, and the New National Champions' in Barry Naughton and Kellee S. Tsai (eds.) *State Capitalism, Institutional Adaptation, and the Chinese Miracle* (Cambridge 2015), 48.
37 Interim Regulation, Article 12.

restructuring of the SOEs; (3) dispatching supervisors to the enterprises in which it invests; (4) appointing, removing, and assessing the principal officials of the SOEs; (5) supervising the value maintaining and increase of the state owned assets in SOEs.[38]

It was noted that the SASAC plays a dual role as an intermediary between the Chinese State and its SOEs. On one hand, the SASAC is an investor that should be interested in the profitability of its assets. On the other hand, as a quasi-governmental body it is responsible for market control and regulation on behalf of the government.[39] The SASAC has overseen the process of SOE consolidation by merging the existing SOEs and building highly integrated SOE groups (Annex I). As a result, the typical Chinese SOE group consists of the core company, which is normally unlisted and wholly owned by the SASAC. The group would also include a 'brand company', which operates as the group's 'face' in dealing with third parties and is frequently listed on stock exchanges.[40] The SOE grouping also often includes a finance or asset management company, a research institute, and numerous vertically integrated subsidiaries engaged in the production and commercialization activities.[41] What differentiates the Chinese SOE groups from other multinational corporations is 'their partial marketization and extremely rapid increase in size and complexity, due to both domestic restructuring and overseas expansion',[42] which exacerbates the problems of efficient oversight, especially in the overseas operations.[43] As noted by Sutherland and Ning, 'pyramids facilitate ownership diversification while maintain control at the apex – in the hand of party and government officials'.[44] It was also noted that the leaders of the central controlling SOEs 'are seldom held accountable for

---

38 Interim Regulation, Article 13.

39 See Yongnian Zheng and Minjia Chen, 'China's State-Owned Enterprise Reform and Its Discontents' (2009) 56 *Problems of Post-Communism* 36.

40 For example, the SASAC controls CNPC, which in turn controls PetroChina, a publicly listed company engaged in domestic and overseas petroleum operations.

41 See Li-Wen Lin, 'A Network Anatomy of Chinese State-Owned Enterprises' (2017a) 16 *World Trade Review* 583, 585–587; Li-Wen Lin and Curtis J. Milhaupt, 'We Are the (National) Champions: Understanding the Mechanisms of State Capitalism in China' (2013) 65 *Stanford Law Review* 697, 716–721.

42 Wendy Leutert, 'Challenges Ahead in China's Reform of State-Owned Enterprises' (2016) 21 *Asia Policy* 83, 96.

43 See Shuping Liao and Yongsheng Zhang, 'A New Context for Managing Overseas Direct Investment by Chinese State-Owned Enterprises' (2014) 7 *China Economic Journal* 126.

44 Dylan Sutherland and Lutao Ning, 'The Emergence and Evolution of Chinese Business Groups: Are Pyramidal Groups Forming?' in Barry Naughton and Kellee S. Tsai (eds.) *State Capitalism, Institutional Adaptation, and the Chinese Miracle* (Cambridge 2015), 140.

the economic performance of their enterprises and their subsidiaries, at least as long as they do not deteriorate too dramatically'.[45]

As a majority shareholder, the SASAC is empowered to appoint and remove the management of the SOEs under its control. The Company Law stipulates that in the wholly owned SOEs, the SASAC appoints the members of the board of directors and designates the chairman and vice-chairman of the board.[46] However, it appears misleading, as the candidates for the board of directors of a centrally owned SOE are nominated by the Central Organization Department of the CPC.[47] This led Lin to conclude that the 'SASAC in reality can only exercise its rights in the shadow of party control'.[48]

When it comes to the board of supervisors, the SASAC serves as the shareholders meeting and appoints the members of the supervisory board along with the assembly of the employee representatives, which is authorized to elect no less than one-third of the supervisory board members.[49] The external members are frequently 'retired government officials, famous economists, lawyers and accountants who have close relationships with the authorities. Second, within those corporations, the secretaries of corporations' disciplinary committees of the CPC and worker representatives constitute internal shareholder supervisors'.[50] The supervisory function is also played by the disciplinary committees of the CPC within the SOEs, which maintain the managerial discipline and ensure the implementation of the state policies.

The corporatization of the Chinese SOEs has increased the number of managers that rely on their professional expertise and the financial performance of the company for promotion. Thus, a study on the basis of careers of 1,250 top executives from 1,084 publicly listed SOEs during 2003–2012 demonstrated the following: (1) more than a third of executives have prior government experience or concurrent political roles; (2) almost one-tenth of executives from provincial SOEs are promoted into government positions; (3) in case of subsidiaries of central SOEs, the executives are increasingly

---

45 Lin Zhang, 'Adaptive Efficiency and the Corporate Governance of Chinese State-Controlled Listed Companies: Evidence from the Fundraising of Chinese Domestic Venture Capital' (2010) 10 *UC Davis Business Law Journal* 151, 159.
46 Company Law, Articles 67–68.
47 See Roman Tomasic, 'Company Law Implementation in the PRC: The Rule of Law in the Shadow of the State' (2015) 15 *Journal of Corporate Law Studies* 285, 299.
48 Lin, 'A Network Anatomy of Chinese State-Owned Enterprises', 588.
49 Company Law, Article 70.
50 Lin Zhang, 'Corporate Governance of Chinese State-Controlled Listed Companies: Evidence from the Exit of Chinese Domestic Venture Capital' (2011) 6 *Frontiers of Law in China* 259, 269–270.

promoted on the basis of financial performance.[51] A study[52] of the career paths of the 113 SOEs under the control of the Central SASAC and the top 100 listed SOE companies revealed the following findings: (1) 92–99% of the CEOs hold CPC membership; (2) these individuals have joined the party ranks at an early age – 25/24 years old; (3) their average age when appointed CEO was 49/47 years; (4) the majority of the CEOs in the listed SOEs have followed single-group career tracks, which 'implies that the SOE management system values group-specific knowledge and gives group insiders promotional advantages';[53] (5) CEOs of the SOEs directly under the control of the Central SASAC have more diverse work experience accumulated in various political and administrative positions. Another study on the remuneration practices in the Chinese state owned banks (Annex I, Table 2) concluded that while remuneration levels remain low, the political promotion remains the most important incentive for the state bankers.[54] These studies indicate that a significant proportion of the senior management in the centrally controlled SOEs have their corporate careers closely linked to political and administrative appointments, which dilutes the possibilities of SASAC of exerting decisive influence over the conduct of the SOE executives.

It should be noted also that the SASAC, as a nominal state shareholder, functions in the regulatory environment characterized by a high degree of decentralization and fragmentation, along with other institutions, often competing for power and influence over the SOEs: regional governments looking after the economic interests of their local constituents and SOEs; the NDRC allocating state investment projects; the MOFCOM overseeing foreign economic relations; state owned banks providing access to project finance; sector-specific regulators, etc.[55] It is therefore not surprising that the SASAC was characterized as lacking 'the necessary political authority to exercise administrative power over the SOEs or curb their monopoly behaviours and other anti-market practices'.[56]

---

51 See Kjeld Erik Brodsgaard, Paul Hubbard, Guilong Cai and Linlin Zhang, 'China's SOE Executives: Drivers of or Obstacles to Reform?' (2017) 35 *Copenhagen Journal of Asian Studies* 52.

52 See Li-Wen Lin, 'Reforming China's State-Owned Enterprises: From Structure to People' (2017) 229 *China Quarterly* 107.

53 Ibid., 118.

54 See Longjie Lu, 'Bankers' Remuneration and Political Incentives in Chinese State-Owned Commercial Banks: Regulation and Practice' (2019) 19 *Journal of Corporate Law Studies* 451, 489.

55 See Lee Jones and Yizhen Zou, 'Rethinking the Role of State-Owned Enterprises in China's Rise' (2017) 22 *New Political Economy* 743, 747.

56 Hong Yu, 'The Ascendency of State-Owned Enterprises in China: Development, Controversy and Problems' (2014) 23 *Journal of Contemporary China* 161, 180.

2.3 Political control: from shadows to the front stage

SOEs' modern corporate system with Chinese features is unique because it incorporates the Party's leadership into all aspects of their corporate governance and Party organizations into the corporate governance structure.[57]

One of the primary channels of the CPC's control over the SOEs is the appointment of the senior management, which depending on the level of the position can be done through the SASAC or directly by the Central Organizational Department of the CPC.[58] Being part of the party's leading cadres, the SOE senior executives can be shifted by the CPC to the leadership positions in the party organizations, government, or other SOEs.[59] It was argued that the CPC membership of the SOE executives has profound effect on their decision making: 'the nomenklatura system prevents business leaders from successfully challenging Party rule and helps to ensure that the achievements and the continued growth of the business sector will benefit the Party and contribute to regime stability'.[60] As a result, the SOE 'managers, aspiring to careers in the Party-state system, will opt for business decisions that they believe serve the Party-state's goals in each context whether or not these align with corporate targets or the wealth of all shareholders'.[61]

The 2015 Guiding Opinions on the SOE reform reaffirmed the political control over the SOEs: 'the Party's leadership over SOEs shall be upheld. This is the political direction and principle that must be held fast to in deepening SOE reform'.[62] They have effectively moved the CPC organs from the background to the front stage of the SOE management: 'the Party organizations of SOEs shall enjoy a more solid statutory position in corporate governance, and fully display their core political role'.[63] The guidelines provide for the integration of the CPC organs into the corporate governance of SOEs: 'include the overall requirements on Party building into the articles of association of SOEs, make clear the statutory role of the Party

---

57 Xi Jinping, *The Governance of China II* (Foreign Languages Press 2017), 193.
58 See Brodsgaard, 'Politics and Business Group Formation in China: The Party in Control?', 633; Wang, 'The Political Logic of Corporate Governance in China's State-Owned Enterprises', 658.
59 See Brodsgaard, 'Politics and Business Group Formation in China: The Party in Control?', 638.
60 Ibid., 645.
61 Tamar Groswald Ozery, 'The Politicization of Corporate Governance: A Viable Alternative?' (SSRN 2019) <https://papers.ssrn.com/sol3/papers.cfm?abstract_id=3608727> accessed 31 July 2020, 21.
62 2015 Guiding Opinions, para 2
63 Ibid., para 3.

organizations of SOEs in their corporate governance structures'.[64] The Company Law now explicitly instructs all companies to provide necessary conditions for the operation of the CPC branches established according to the CPC Constitution.[65]

This integration of the CPC organs into the corporate governance of the SOEs will be achieved by the so-called 'two-way access and cross-representation', which provides for the dual roles of the SOE executives combining their corporate and political responsibilities: 'in principle, a SOE shall set the position of the chairman of the board of directors separately from the position of the general manager, and its Party secretary and chairman of the board of directors shall generally be served by the same person'.[66] The CPC members will qualify for the positions in the board of supervisors, board of directors, and management, while the persons that occupy those corporate positions will join the party ranks. According to the CPC regulations, the secretary of the SOE party branch and the position of the chairman of the board of directors should be held by the same person.[67] Similarly, the general manager of the SOE should simultaneously serve as a deputy secretary of the party organization in the SOE. The regulations explicitly prescribe that members of the party organization's leadership who enter the board of directors, board of supervisors, and the management must follow the party organization's decisions.[68] These double appointments combined with the frequent rotations of senior management among various SOEs within certain industry sectors limit the latter's ability to establish strong autonomous networks and make them more dependent on the political decisions concerning their placement and promotion.[69]

Groswald Ozery refers to the legalization of the role of the party organizations within SOEs as 'politicization of corporate governance' whereby the CPC 'itself, beyond any traditional shareholder role the state may have, becomes a legal corporate constituent with unique interests and a distinct capacity to convey, direct, and monitor the ways these interests will be pursued'.[70] The integration of the party control into the existing corporate bodies is achieved in the following ways: (1) party committee is granted authority in respect

64 Ibid., para 24.
65 Company Law, Article 19.
66 2015 Guiding Opinions, para 24.
67 Regulations of the Communist Party of China on the Work of Party Organizations in the State-Owned Enterprises (29 November 2019), Article 14.
68 Ibid., Article 14.
69 See Wendy Leutert, 'Firm Control: Governing the State-Owned Economy under Xi Jinping' (2018) 1–2 *China Perspectives* 27, 30.
70 Groswald Ozery T., 'The Politicization of Corporate Governance: A Viable Alternative?' 28–29.

to personnel management; (2) cross-representation of board members and supervisory committee members in the party committee; (3) party committee is designated as internal governing body with an authority to oversee, audit, and assess major corporate decisions.[71]

On 29 November 2019, the Political Bureau of the CPC Central Committee approved CPC regulations on the work of party organizations in the SOEs.[72] These regulations require the CPC membership to 'persist in strengthening the party's leadership and improve corporate governance, and integrate party leadership into all aspects of corporate governance'.[73] The regulations explicitly require that the status, powers, and procedures of the CPC committees should be included in the articles of association of the respective SOEs in order to ensure that the discussion within the party organization is a prerequisite for taking any major decision by the board of directors or the management.[74] Such major decisions include among others: (1) major measures implementing the decisions of the CPC Central Committee and the national development strategies; (2) SOE development strategies, mid-term and long-term development plans, important reform plans; (3) decisions concerning corporate asset reorganizations, property right transfers, and large investment decisions; (4) changes in the corporate structure of the SOEs, development and adoption of important rules and regulations; (5) major matters involving safety of production and maintenance, employees' rights and interests, as well as SOE's social responsibilities.[75]

The CPC branches in the SOEs have, among others, the following duties: (1) to 'implement the party's line, guidelines, and policies, and supervise and ensure that major decision-making arrangements of the party's central and higher-level party organization resolutions are implemented in this enterprise'; (2) to 'study and discuss major business management matters of the enterprise, and support the shareholders' meeting, the board of directors, the board of supervisors and the management to exercise their powers according to law'; (3) to 'strengthen the leadership and control over the selection and employment of enterprises, and build the leadership team and the cadre and talent teams of the company';[76] (4) to 'supervise party members, cadres and other employees of the enterprise . . . and safeguard the

---

71 Ibid., 26–27.
72 Regulations of the Communist Party of China on the Work of Party Organizations in the State-Owned Enterprises (29 November 2019).
73 Ibid., Article 3(1).
74 Ibid., Article 13.
75 Ibid., Article 15.
76 Ibid., Article 11.

interests of the country, the collective, and the masses'.[77] The Chinese policy makers are well aware of the practical difficulties of integrating political leadership and autonomous decision making on commercial matters into the corporate governance system of the SOEs:

> We still need to explore how we can seamlessly integrate the corporate governance standard system with the unique mechanisms of SOEs, including the CPC's supervisory role in the management of SOE officials, the decisive role of the CPC committee in decision making, and SASAC's direct management of business matters of SOEs.[78]

More pessimistic voices also cautioned that 'it will be difficult for companies to avoid Party or government interference and establish the market-disciplined and market-directed corporate governance structure required to improve their efficiency and profit-making ability'.[79]

Finally, the role of the CPC has also been 'legalized' in relation to the anti-corruption enforcement, which has been centralized under the CPC-led National Supervisory Commission (NSC).[80] The NSC has absorbed the Ministry of Supervision and the Bureau of Corruption Prevention, previously under the State Council, thus further strengthening party control over public administration.[81] Although, initially, the party discipline was entrusted to the Central Commission for Disciplinary Inspection and applied to the party members, the newly created NSC has extended its disciplinary authority over all public servants including the SOE managers.[82]

2.4 Mergers of state owned enterprises under China's anti-monopoly law

> *Taming the Chinese leviathan through antitrust law is unfortunately a false hope for future reform of Chinese SOEs.*[83]

---

77 Ibid., Article 12(5).
78 Changwen Zhao and Yongwei Zhang, 'Several Major Issues on Deepening State-Owned Enterprises Reform' (2015) 8 *China Economic Journal* 143, 150.
79 Hong Yu, 'Reform of State-Owned Enterprises in China: The Chinese Communist Party Strikes Back' (2019) 43 *Asian Studies Review* 332, 346.
80 Supervision Law of the People's Republic of China, Article 7.
81 See Nis Grünberg and Katja Drinhausen, 'The Party Leads on Everything: China's Changing Governance in Xi Jinping's New Era' (Mercator Institute for China Studies 2019) <https://merics.org/en/report/party-leads-everything> accessed 31 July 2020, 7.
82 Supervision Law, Article 15.
83 Angela Huyue Zhang, 'Taming the Chinese Leviathan: Is Antitrust Regulation a False Hope?' (2015) 51 *Stanford Journal of International Law* 195, 228.

Although the aforementioned legal and policy documents emphasize the CPC leadership over the SOEs and the latter's role in implementing the industrial policy and other public policies in China, externally the Chinese government has consistently emphasized the autonomy of the SOEs in their commercial operations. For example, in 2017, a centrally controlled SOE, China National Coal Corporation attempted to invoke sovereign immunity against a private claim for the breach of contract before the Court of First Instance of Hong Kong SAR. The court had to establish whether the SOE should be viewed as a part of the state (PRC), which would make it immune from the civil litigation. The relevant factors that would determine the SOE's status as a part of the state were: (1) independent discretion enjoyed by the SOE; (2) control exercised by the state as investor; (3) separate legal personality of the SOE; (4) the power of the state to appoint and remove senior officers of the SOE; (5) the financial autonomy of the SOE.[84] Upon the request of the Hong Kong Department of Justice requesting the opining of the Central Government, the Hong Kong and Macao Affairs Office of the State Council has produced the following explanation:

> China National Coal Group Corporation is a wholly state-owned enterprise, an enterprise legal person, established according to the law. According to the relevant legal regulations of our country, a state-owned enterprise is an independent legal entity, which carries out activities of production and operation on its own, independently assumes legal liabilities, and there is no special legal person status or legal interests superior to other enterprises. In the Mainland or in foreign states, all state-owned enterprises of our country respond to litigation arising from their activities of production and operation in the capacity of independent legal persons. Therefore, save for extremely extraordinary circumstances where the conduct was performed on behalf of the state via appropriate authorisation, etc, the state-owned enterprises of our country when carrying out commercial activities shall not be deemed as a part of the Central Government, and shall not be deemed as a body performing functions on behalf of the Central Government. It should be pointed out that the opinion above shall not be interpreted as derogation of any rights and immunity enjoyed according to law by the Central Government and its bodies in the Hong Kong SAR.[85]

---

84 TNB Fuel Services SDN BHD v China National Coal Group Corp [2017] 3 HKC 588, para 4.
85 Ibid., para 14.

In this case, the Hong Kong court has refused the SOE's request for sovereign immunity since

> it is apparent from the Assets Law and from the Articles of the respondent that it is able to use, profit from and dispose of its property, and to use its annual profits and common reserves to cover its own losses and to expand its business.[86]

The control exercised by the SASAC through appointments and removal of the SOE's management 'was not considered by the court to be sufficient to render a corporation an agent of the Crown to be entitled to immunity'.[87] The Chinese government's position in the case reflects its general stance on the separation between the state and its SOEs in relation to the latter's commercial transactions.[88] This position becomes especially pronounced in cases concerning the determination of the 'public body' under the WTO rules and national trade defense mechanisms, which may lead to imposition of countervailing duties on the products affected by subsidies coming from the SOEs and state owned banks (Annex I, Table 2).[89]

Following its firm stance on the separation of the state and its SOEs in international economic law, China maintains a similar approach in its domestic legislation, particularly in relation to the SOEs' conduct as market players under competition law. China's anti-monopoly law (AML) regards SOEs as 'business operators' and subjects them to both antitrust and merger control enforcement.[90] The AML also stipulates that

> [w]ith respect to the industries controlled by the State-owned economy and concerning the lifeline of national economy and national security or the industries lawfully enjoying exclusive production and sales, the State shall protect these lawful business operations conducted by the business operators therein, and shall supervise and control these

---

86 Ibid., para 84.
87 Ibid., para 85. See also Liying Zhang and Kuan Shang, 'The Crown in the People's Republic: Chinese State Entities Enjoying Crown Immunity in Hong Kong' (2012) 9 *Manchester Journal of International Economic Law* 45.
88 See Dahai Qi, 'State Immunity, China, and Its Shifting Position' (2008) 7 *Chinese Journal of International Law* 307, 315.
89 See Ru Ding, 'Public Body' or Not: Chinese State-Owned Enterprise' (2014) 48 *Journal of World Trade* 167.
90 Anti-Monopoly Law of the People's Republic of China, issued 30 August 2007, effective 1 August 2008, Article 12. The term 'business operator' extends to any 'natural person, legal person, or any other organization that engages in the production or business of commodities or provides services'.

business operations and the prices of these commodities and services provided by these business operators.[91]

In practice, the preceding provision has resulted in rare instances of antitrust investigations involving SOEs.[92] In relation to the merger control, Zhang argued that the MOFCOM's lenience in tolerating the failure to notify the SOE-related concentrations should be explained by the selective enforcement of the AML rather than its inapplicability to the SOEs.[93]

The merger control provisions of the AML contain the definition of 'concentration of business operators', which is equivalent to the EU definition of concentration under the EUMR. The AML distinguishes the following types of concentrations: (1) merger of business operators; (2) control over a business operator gained by another business operator through acquiring shares or assets; (3) control over a business operator or the ability of exerting a decisive influence on the same gained by another business operator through contracts or other means.[94] If a concentration reaches the set turnover thresholds,[95] it is subject to notification and cannot be implemented prior to the decision to be issued by the SAMR (formerly the Anti-Monopoly Bureau of the MOFCOM).[96] However, the following situations are regarded as internal reorganization, which are not subject to an obligation to notify: (1) one of the business operators involved in the concentration owns 50% or more of the voting shares or assets of each of the other business operators; or (2) one and the same business operator not involved in the concentration owns 50% or more of the voting shares or assets of each of the business operators involved in the concentration.[97]

---

91 AML, Article 7.
92 See Sarah Wersborg, 'Anti-Monopoly Law in China: Administrative and Private Enforcement and the Belt and Road Initiative from an Anti-Monopoly Law Perspective' in Yun Zhao (ed.) *International Governance and the Rule of Law in China under the Belt and Road Initiative* (Cambridge 2018), 100.
93 Angela Huyue Zhang, 'The Single-Entity Theory: An Antitrust Time Bomb for Chinese State-Owned Enterprises' (2012) 8 *Journal of Competition Law and Economics* 805, 826.
94 AML, Article 20.
95 State Council, Provisions on the Standard for Declaration of Concentration of Business Operators (8 March 2008), Article 3: (1) the worldwide turnover of all undertakings involved in the concentration exceeds CNY 10 billion in the last accounting year, and the turnover in China of at least two undertakings involved exceeds CNY 400 million each in the last accounting year; (2) the turnover in China of all the undertakings involved in the concentration exceeds CNY 2 billion in the last accounting year, and the turnover in China of at least two undertakings involved exceeds CNY 400 million each in the last accounting year.
96 AML, Article 21.
97 Ibid., Article 22.

Although the AML introduced administrative fines for the failure to notify economic concentrations, the maximum penalty of CNY 500,000 can hardly achieve an effective deterrence.[98] The MOFCOM has routinely sanctioned both private parties and SOEs for the failure to notify, but the penalties rarely reached the maximum permitted by law.[99] The highest fine of CNY 400,000 was imposed on the Swedish company Bombardier Transportation in 2016 for the failure to notify its joint venture with New United Group Co. Ltd.[100] In January 2020, the SAMR published the proposed amendments to the AML, which proposed to raise the fines for failure to notify by setting their maximum amount at 10% of the annual turnover of the business operator concerned.[101] In the meantime, the SAMR has continued applying administrative penalties for the failure to notify.[102] In 2018–2019, SAMR sanctioned several SOEs for the failure to notify their concentrations, including Guangzhou Steel Holding Co. Ltd.,[103] Harbin Electric Co. Ltd.,[104] China Post Capital Management Co. Ltd.,[105] Guangxi Liuzhou Iron and Steel (Group) Co.,[106] BAIC Motor Co. Ltd.,[107] Shanghai Xingfu Motorcycle Co.

---

98 Ibid., Article 48.
99 See MOFCOM decisions 788/2014 of 2 December 2014 (CNY 300,000); 668/2015 of 15 September 2015 (CNY 150,000); 669/2015 of 16 September 2015 (CNY 200,000); 670/2015 of 16 September 2015 (CNY 150,000); 671/2015 of 16 September 2015 (CNY 200,000); 173/2016 of 21 April 2016 (CNY 150,000); 174/2016 of 21 April 2016 (CNY 300,000 and 400,000); 175/2016 of 21 April 2016 (CNY 150,000); 965/2016 of 16 December 2016 (CNY 300,000); 681/2016 of 31 August 2016 (CNY 150,000); 682/2016 of 31 August 2016 (CNY 200,000); 6/2017 of 9 January 2017 (CNY 150,000); 171/2017 of 21 April 2017 (CNY 150,000); 205/2017 of 5 May 2017 (CNY 150,000); 206/2017 of 5 May 2017 (CNY 300,000); 408/2017 of 14 July 2017 (CNY 150,000); 410/2017 of 11 July 2017 (CNY 150,000); 12/2018 of 10 January 2018 (CNY 300,000); 32/2018 of 19 January 2018 (CNY 150,000); 33/2018 of 19 January 2018 (CNY 300,000); 129/2018 of 4 April 2018 (CNY 200,000); 130/2018 of 4 April 2018 (CNY 200,000).
100 MOFCOM decision 174/2016 of 21 April 2016.
101 The draft amendments have been published by SAMR on 2 January 2020 at <www.samr. gov.cn/hd/zjdc/202001/t20200102_310120.html> accessed 31 July 2020.
102 See SAMR decisions 20/2018 of 21 December 2018 (CNY 400,000); 1/2019 of 14 February 2019 (CNY 300,000); 2/2019 of 19 February 2019 (CNY 200,000); 3/2019 of 19 February 2019 (CNY 300,000); 8/2019 of 28 April 2019 (CNY 300,000); 19/2019 of 25 June 2019 (CNY 300,000); 37/2019 of 16 August 2019 (CNY 300,00); 41/2019 of 16 September 2019 (CNY 300,000); 43/2019 of 29 September 2019 (CNY 300,000); 44/2019 of 29 September 2019 (CNY 300,000); 50/2019 of 13 December 2019 (CNY 400,000); 51/2019 of 20 December 2019 (CNY 350,000).
103 SAMR decision 16/2018 of 4 December 2018 (CNY 300,000).
104 SAMR decision 38/2019 of 3 September 2019 (CNY 300,000).
105 SAMR decision 40/2019 of 16 September 2019 (CNY 400,000).
106 SAMR decision 42/2019 of 16 September 2019 (CNY 350,000).
107 SAMR decision 45/2019 of 27 September 2019 (CNY 300,000).

Ltd.,[108] Liaoning Port Group Co. Ltd.,[109] and Guangzhou Port Co. Ltd.[110] Although the SOEs are regarded as business operators under the AML and have been routinely penalized for the failure to notify their concentrations prior to the implementation, the MOFCOM's clearance decisions provide little information on the substantive assessment of those mergers. Nevertheless, the handling of the concentrations involving the centrally controlled SOEs helps to understand the role of the merger control in the consolidation of the SOE sector in China.

In 2015, China moved to merge its maritime shipping SOEs China Ocean Shipping (Group) Corporation and China Shipping (Group) Corporation into a newly established entity – China COSCO Shipping Corporation. On 11 December 2015, the Central SASAC announced the State Council's approval of the proposed merger.[111] The SOE-to-SOE merger was notified to the MOFCOM and obtained clearance on 4 February 2016.[112] On the next day, 5 February 2016, the establishment of COSCO was entered into the company register. The year 2015 also saw the consolidation of the railway manufacturing companies China CNR Corporation and China South Railway Group into CRRC Corporation. CNR announced that the proposed SOE-to-SOE merger received the approval of the State Council and the SASAC on 5 March 2015. The clearance decision of the MOFCOM was announced on 21 September 2015.[113] However, by June 2015 the CNR had implemented changes in its corporate registration, including the name of the newly created SOE, the shareholders and legal representatives, etc.

In 2016, the consolidation of the SOEs sector in the steel industry led to the acquisition by Baoshan Iron and Steel Co. Ltd. of Wuhan Iron and Steel Co. Ltd. (WISCO), both under the control of the Central SASAC. The SASAC announced that the State Council had approved the proposed consolidation on 22 September 2016.[114] The MOFCOM subsequently issued an unconditional clearance of the notified concentration on 30 November 2016.[115] However, Baosteel already moved to implement the corporate changes, such

---

108 SAMR decision 46/2019 of 1 November 2019 (CNY 350,000).
109 SAMR decision 48/2019 of 9 December 2019 (CNY 350,000).
110 SAMR decision 49/2019 of 9 December 2019 (CNY 300,000).
111 SASAC, China Ocean Shipping (Group) Corporation and China Shipping (Group) Corporation implement reorganization (11 December 2015) <www.sasac.gov.cn/n2588030/n2588924/c4297095/content.html> accessed 31 July 2020.
112 MOFCOM decision 32/2016 of 4 February 2016.
113 MOFCOM decision 68/2015 of 21 September 2015.
114 The joint reorganization of Baosteel and WISCO was approved (22 September 2016), <www.gov.cn/xinwen/2016-09/22/content_5110905.htm> accessed 31 July 2020.
115 MOFCOM decision 53/2016 of 30 November 2016.

as names, legal representatives, articles of association, etc., on 17 November 2016, which preceded the announcement of MOFCOM's clearance decision. In 2017, China National Building Material Co. Ltd. (CNBM) was set to absorb another SOE, China National Materials Co. Ltd. (Sinoma). On 23 November 2017, the two companies announced that the Central SASAC, as their controlling shareholder, had approved the proposed merger.[116] The concentration was notified to the MOFCOM and received clearance on 19 December 2017.[117] Following the MOFCOM's merger clearance, CNBM registered the increase of its share capital and the changes in the management in July 2018.

These four examples of the SOE-to-SOE concentrations demonstrate that at least formally these transactions are regarded as 'concentration of business operators' under the AML even though the controlling shareholder, the Central SASAC, retains its control over the newly created or reorganized SOE post-merger. The clearance announcements do not reveal the competitive assessment of the notified concentrations by the MOFCOM. Nevertheless, the pattern of implementing these concentrations indicates that once the decision on an SOE's reorganization has been taken by the State Council and publicly announced, the clearance of the MOFCOM remains a formality. The limited importance of the MOFCOM's involvement also can be reflected by the fact that at least in two cases, *CNR/CSR* and *Baosteel/ WISCO*, the implementation of the reorganization may have occurred prior to the merger clearance by the MOFCOM. It was also reported that the SOE merger of China Unicom and Netcom in 2008, although meeting the notification thresholds under the AML, was not notified to the MOFCOM and no punitive action was taken in that regard by the ministry.[118]

Bibliography

Bath V, 'Chinese Companies and Outbound Investment: The Balance between Domestic and International Concerns' in Lisa Toohey, Colin B Picker, Jonathan Greenacre (eds.) *China in the International Economic Order: New Directions and Changing Paradigms* (Cambridge, 2015).

Brodsgaard KE, 'Politics and Business Group Formation in China: The Party in Control?' (2012) 211 *China Quarterly* 624.

Brodsgaard KE, P Hubbard, G Cai, L Zhang, 'China's SOE Executives: Drivers of or Obstacles to Reform?' (2017) 35 *Copenhagen Journal of Asian Studies* 52.

---

116 Joint announcement on CNBM/Sinoma merger (23 November 2017) <www.cnbmltd. com/old_2018//20171124084744946.pdf> accessed 31 July 2020.

117 MOFCOM decision 64/2017 of 19 December 2017.

118 See Zhang, 'Taming the Chinese Leviathan: Is Antitrust Regulation a False Hope?', 216.

Che L, 'Legal Implications of the Deepened Reform of Chinese State-Owned Enterprises: What Can Be Expected from Recent Reforms?' (2016) 8 *Tsinghua China Law Review* 171.

Ding R, '"Public Body" or Not: Chinese State-Owned Enterprise' (2014) 48 *Journal of World Trade* 167.

Du M, 'When China's National Champions Go Global: Nothing to Fear but Fear Itself?' (2014) 48 *Journal of World Trade* 1127.

Guo R, 'The Creation of Modern State Ownership: Legal Transplantation and the Rise of Modern State-Owned Big Businesses in China' (2013) 4 *Peking University Journal of Legal Studies* 69.

Groswald Ozery T, 'The Politicization of Corporate Governance: A Viable Alternative?' (SSRN, 2019) <https://papers.ssrn.com/sol3/papers.cfm?abstract_id=3608727> accessed 31 July 2020.

Grünberg N, K Drinhausen, 'The Party Leads on Everything: China's Changing Governance in Xi Jinping's New Era' (Mercator Institute for China Studies, 2019) <https://merics.org/en/report/party-leads-everything> accessed 31 July 2020.

Holbig H, 'The Party and Private Entrepreneurs in the PRC' (2002) 16 *Copenhagen Journal of Asian Studies* 30.

Jones L, Y Zou, 'Rethinking the Role of State-Owned Enterprises in China's Rise' (2017) 22 *New Political Economy* 743.

Leutert W, 'Challenges Ahead in China's Reform of State-Owned Enterprises' (2016) 21 *Asia Policy* 83.

———, 'Firm Control: Governing the State-Owned Economy under Xi Jinping' (2018) 1–2 *China Perspectives* 27.

Li X, KE Brodsgaard, 'SOE Reform in China: Past, Present and Future' (2013) 31 *Copenhagen Journal of Asian Studies* 54.

Liao S, Y Zhang, 'A New Context for Managing Overseas Direct Investment by Chinese State-Owned Enterprises' (2014) 7 *China Economic Journal* 126.

Lin JY, F Cai, Z Li, 'Competition, Policy Burdens, and State-Owned Enterprise Reform' (1998) 88 *AEA Papers and Proceedings* 422.

Lin LW, 'A Network Anatomy of Chinese State-Owned Enterprises' (2017) 16 *World Trade Review* 583.

———, 'Reforming China's State-Owned Enterprises: From Structure to People' (2017) 229 *China Quarterly* 107.

Lin LW, CJ Milhaupt, 'We Are the (National) Champions: Understanding the Mechanisms of State Capitalism in China' (2013) 65 *Stanford Law Review* 697.

Lu L, 'Bankers' Remuneration and Political Incentives in Chinese State-Owned Commercial Banks: Regulation and Practice' (2019) 19 *Journal of Corporate Law Studies* 451.

Naughton B, 'The Transformation of the State Sector: SASAC, the Market Economy, and the New National Champions' in Barry Naughton, Kellee S Tsai (eds.) *State Capitalism, Institutional Adaptation, and the Chinese Miracle* (Cambridge, 2015).

Pearson MM, 'State-Owned Business and Party-State Regulation in China's Modern Political Economy' in Barry Naughton, Kellee S Tsai (eds.) *State Capitalism, Institutional Adaptation, and the Chinese Miracle* (Cambridge, 2015).

Sutherland D, L Ning, 'The Emergence and Evolution of Chinese Business Groups: Are Pyramidal Groups Forming?' in Barry Naughton, Kellee S Tsai (eds.) *State Capitalism, Institutional Adaptation, and the Chinese Miracle* (Cambridge, 2015).

Qi D, 'State Immunity, China, and Its Shifting Position' (2008) 7 *Chinese Journal of International Law* 307.

Tomasic R, 'Company Law Implementation in the PRC: The Rule of Law in the Shadow of the State' (2015) 15 *Journal of Corporate Law Studies* 285.

Wang J, 'The Political Logic of Corporate Governance in China's State-Owned Enterprises' (2014) 47 *Cornell International Law Journal* 631.

Wang Z, 'Corporate Governance Under State Control: The Chinese Experience' (2012) 13 *Theoretical Inquiries in Law* 487.

Wersborg S, 'Anti-Monopoly Law in China: Administrative and Private Enforcement and the Belt and Road Initiative from an Anti-Monopoly Law Perspective' in Yun Zhao (ed.) *International Governance and the Rule of Law in China under the Belt and Road Initiative* (Cambridge, 2018).

Wu M, 'The China, Inc. Challenge to Global Trade Governance' (2016) 57 *Harvard International Law Journal* 261.

Yang K, 'State-Owned Enterprise Reform in Post-Mao China' (2007) 31 *International Journal of Public Administration* 24.

Yu H, 'The Ascendency of State-Owned Enterprises in China: Development, Controversy and Problems' (2014) 23 *Journal of Contemporary China* 161.

———, 'Reform of State-Owned Enterprises in China: The Chinese Communist Party Strikes Back' (2019) 43 *Asian Studies Review* 332.

Zeng P, 'The Establishment of the Socialist Market Economy' (2012) 4(3) *Qiushi Journal* <http://english.qstheory.cn/magazine/201203/201210/t20121008_185077.htm> accessed 31 July 2020.

Zenglein MJ, A Holzmann, 'Evolving Made in China 2025: China's Industrial Policy in the Quest for Global Teach Leadership' (Mercator Institute for China Studies, 2019) <https://merics.org/en/report/evolving-made-china-2025> accessed 31 July 2020.

Zhang AH, 'The Single-Entity Theory: An Antitrust Time Bomb for Chinese State-Owned Enterprises' (2012) 8 *Journal of Competition Law and Economics* 805.

———, 'Taming the Chinese Leviathan: Is Antitrust Regulation a False Hope?' (2015) 51 *Stanford Journal of International Law* 195.

Zhang L, 'Adaptive Efficiency and the Corporate Governance of Chinese State-Controlled Listed Companies: Evidence from the Fundraising of Chinese Domestic Venture Capital' (2010) 10 *UC Davis Business Law Journal* 151.

———, 'Corporate Governance of Chinese State-Controlled Listed Companies: Evidence from the Exit of Chinese Domestic Venture Capital' (2011) 6 *Frontiers of Law in China* 259.

Zhang L, K Shang, 'The Crown in the People's Republic: Chinese State Entities Enjoying Crown Immunity in Hong Kong' (2012) 9 *Manchester Journal of International Economic Law* 45.

Zhao C, Y Zhang, 'Several Major Issues on Deepening State-Owned Enterprises Reform' (2015) 8 *China Economic Journal* 143.

Zheng Y, M Chen, 'China's State-Owned Enterprise Reform and Its Discontents' (2009) 56 *Problems of Post-Communism* 36.

Zhou W, H Gao, X Bai, 'Building a Market Economy Through WTO-Inspired Reform of State-Owned Enterprises in China' (2019) 68 *International and Comparative Law Quarterly* 977.

3 Economic concentrations of China's state owned enterprises under the EU merger control regime

3.1 Chinese SOEs and 'novel legal issues of a general interest'

In the cases that we have examined, we have used the same criteria we adopt to assess mergers involving companies controlled by the Member States.[1]

As demonstrated in Chapter 1, the enforcement practice of applying the EU merger control rules to the SOE-related concentrations has been developed by the European Commission in merger cases mainly involving the EU/EEA-based SOEs.[2] As a result, the Commission's prior merger control practice may have been shaped by the regulatory and corporate governance frameworks within which these companies operate. The principle of competitive neutrality, enforcement of antitrust rules, and state aid law in these jurisdictions have conditioned the approximation of the SOEs' governance and commercial practices to those of the private companies. The exercise of the state control, decisive influence on the decision making of the SOEs, and the possibility to coordinate their conduct on the markets may have also been conditioned by the aforementioned factors. The regulatory environment and the corporate governance of the Chinese SOEs, as described in Chapter 2, present a number of notable differences, which make the application of the elaborated tests and concepts of merger control a challenging endeavor. The present chapter will analyze these challenges and the ways the Commission has dealt with them in its merger assessment practice.

1 Joaquin Almunia, Vice President of the European Commission responsible for Competition Policy, Recent Developments and Future Priorities in EU Competition Policy, International Competition Law Forum St. Gallen, 8 April 2011, SPEECH/11/243 (8 April 2011), <https://ec.europa.eu/commission/presscorner/detail/en/SPEECH_11_243> accessed 31 July 2020.
2 These included Austria (M.5861), Belgium (M.6812), Finland (M.931), France (M.5549), Germany (M.5508), Norway (M.1573), Poland (M.6683, M.9626, M.9014).

Although during the last decade (2010–2020), the Commission has examined around 40 mergers involving Chinese SOEs (Annex II), the majority of these concentrations have been cleared under a simplified procedure. According to the Commission's practice, 'certain categories of notified concentrations are normally cleared without having raised any substantive doubts, provided that there were no special circumstances'.[3] In such cases, the Commission adopts its short-form non-opposition decision under Article 6(1)(b) EUMR under a simplified procedure within 25 working days from the date of notification.[4] According to the Commission's Notice, the short-form decisions should contain the names of the parties, their country of origin, nature of the concentration and economic sectors concerned, as well as a statement that the concentration is declared compatible with the internal market because it falls within one or more of the categories described in the Notice.[5] These categories refer to certain market share or turnover thresholds of the undertakings concerned within the EU internal market.[6] Since at the time of notification, the Chinese SOEs have not yet acquired substantial presence on the EU markets, the notified concentrations qualified for clearance under the simplified procedure.

The short-form clearance decisions normally do not include a detailed description of the relevant market or the anticipated market conduct of the merging parties. For example, in a 2010 decision concerning the state owned airline Air China, controlled by the Central SASAC, the Commission noted that Air China's subsidiary Shenzhen Airlines provided air cargo services from the Pearl Delta region along with the Cathay Pacific Airways.[7] However, the decision does not contain any assessment of the coordination with other state owned airlines, such as China Southern and China Eastern, both controlled by the Central SASAC. In 2011, the Commission has received a merger notification, which concerned an acquisition of control by one Chinese SOE over another Chinese SOE.[8] The

---

3 Commission Notice on a simplified procedure for treatment of certain concentrations under Council Regulation (EC) No 139/2004, OJ C366/5, 14 December 2013, para 1.
4 Ibid., para 2.
5 Ibid., para 27.
6 Ibid., paras 5–6. For joint venture: turnover less than EUR 100 million within the EEA and the total assets transferred to the joint venture is less than EUR 100 million within the EEA. For mergers and acquisitions: combined market share of the parties in horizontal relationship is less than 20%, for vertical relationship – less than 30%. For markets with low degree of concentration (HHI is below 150): combined market share of the parties in horizontal relationship is less than 50%.
7 *Cathay Pacific Airways/Air China/ACC* (Case No. COMP/M.5841) [2010] OJ C208/3, decision of 17 June 2010.
8 *AVIC/Pacific Century Motors* (Case No. COMP/M.6142) [2011] OJ C94/2, decision of 21 March 2011.

acquiring undertaking was AVIC Automobile Industry Co., Ltd., a wholly owned subsidiary of Aviation Industry Corporation of China (AVIC). AVIC is an aerospace and defense conglomerate under the control of the Central SASAC. The target undertaking was Pacific Century Motors Co., Ltd., a company under control of Beijing E-Town, an investment company of the Beijing municipal government, established in 1994 to foster technological development in the city. Since the merger was examined under the simplified procedure, the Commission's clearance decision does not contain any assessment of the corporate governance characteristics of the undertakings involved. In 2017, in a merger case involving Chinese shipping company COSCO, the Commission acknowledged that COSCO was controlled by the Central SASAC but the decision does not contain any further assessment on this issue.[9]

Although the short-form clearance decisions normally do not include a detailed competitive assessment, the Commission's Notice specified that 'to the extent that concentrations involve novel legal issues of a general interest, the Commission would normally abstain from adopting short-form decisions, and would normally revert to a normal first phase merger procedure'.[10] In the case of merger clearance decisions involving Chinese SOEs the Commission opted for a middle ground approach – it has included a more detailed assessment of the 'novel legal issues of a general interest' addressing the specific features of the merging parties and their relationship with the Chinese State. The ensuing discussion is based on the analysis of the Commission's approach exhibited in such non-opposition decisions.

3.2 Looking for a 'single economic unit' among the Chinese SOEs: initial approach

> *When we look at individual cases and the Commission takes decisions on them, competition enforcement follows its own principles and rules – and they are cast in stone: it must be impartial; it must be blind to the nationality of the companies we investigate; and it must be impeccable – if only because practically every decision we take must pass the muster of the European Court.*[11]

---

9 *COSCO Shipping/OOIL* (Case No. COMP/M.8594) [2017] OJ C79/2, decision of 5 December 2017.

10 Ibid., para 8.

11 Margrethe Vestager, 'The Future of Competition', Foreign Policy Association, New York (1 October 2015) <https://wayback.archive-it.org/12090/20191129201809/https://ec.europa.eu/commission/commissioners/2014-2019/vestager/announcements/future-competition_en> accessed 31 July 2020.

The first decision, where the corporate governance of the Chinese SOEs has presented regulatory hurdles for the EU merger control, was the 2011 acquisition by Bluestar, a subsidiary of China National Chemical Corporation (ChemChina) of Elkem AS, a Norwegian company active in the production of silicon-related materials and carbon products.[12] Although the aggregate turnover of both ChemChina and Elkem exceeded the 'Community dimension' thresholds under the EUMR,[13] the Commission focused its assessment on the independence of ChemChina from the Central SASAC, its controlling shareholder, which at that time also controlled more than 125 centrally managed SOEs.

The Commission made reference to its earlier merger decisions involving European SOEs[14] and summarized its approach as determining 'the possible power of the State to influence the companies' commercial strategy and the likelihood for the State to actually coordinate their commercial conduct, either by imposing or facilitating such coordination'.[15] In order to estimate the possibility of the Central SASAC to coordinate the behavior of the SOEs under its control, the Commission has also applied the criteria previously used in SOE-related merger cases: (1) the degree of interlocking directorships between entities owned by the same entity and (2) the existence of adequate safeguards ensuring that commercially sensitive information is not shared between such undertakings.[16]

The merging parties have argued in their submissions that apart from nominating the management of ChemChina, the Central SASAC 'does not interfere with the strategic decision-making of ChemChina, such as approval of the business plan or budget'.[17] However, because the Chinese SOEs accounted only for a small (10–20%) share of the silicon production, the Commission considered that it was not necessary to reach any definitive conclusions on the subject of ChemChina's independence

---

12 *China National Bluestar/Elkem* (Case No. COMP/M.6082) [2011] OJ C274/7, decision of 31 March 2011. See also Frederic Depoortere, 'The EU Commission Clears in Phase I A Merger in the Silicon Sector Examining Possible Coordination by the Chinese State of Market Behaviour of Chinese State-Owned Companies (*China National Bluestar/Elkem*)' (2011) *e-Competitions Bulletin* March 2011, Art. N° 38917 <www.concurrences.com/en/bulletin/news-issues/march-2011/The-EU-Commission-clears-in-phase> accessed 31 July 2020.

13 Ibid., para 6.

14 *Soffin/Hypo Real Estate* (Case No. COMP/M.5508) [2009] OJ C147/8, decision of 14 May 2009; *Republic of Austria/Hypo Group Alpe Adria* (Case No. COMP/M.5861) [2010] OJ C236/1, decision of 4 August 2010; *Neste/IVO* (Case No. IV/M.931) [1998] OJ C218/4, decision of 2 June 1998.

15 *China National Bluestar/Elkem*, para 10.

16 Ibid., para 11.

17 Ibid., para 19.

from the Central SASAC: 'the proposed transaction would not lead to any competition concerns even if all other SOEs in the markets concerned under Central SASAC were to be regarded as one economic entity'.[18] The anti-competitive scenarios, such as horizontal collusion or vertical foreclosure were unlikely due to the absence of sufficient market power of the Chinese SOEs on the relevant markets.

The Commission has also addressed the question of whether SOEs controlled by the Central SASAC and those owned by the regional SASACs should be considered as part of a single economic unit. The merging parties have advanced the following arguments against such conclusion: (1) regional SASACs are owned by regional/provincial/municipal governments and are not supposed to act in the interest of the central government; (2) management appointments made by regional SASACs are not coordinated with the Central SASAC; (3) there is no direct command relationship between the Central SASAC and regional SASACs; (4) in their management of SOEs, the Central SASAC and regional SASACs pursue different objectives and strategies; (5) there are significant differences between the strategies of different regional SASACs.[19] On the basis of the preceding, the Commission concluded that at least in the silicon and carbon industry there is 'no indication that Regional SASACs and the SOEs under their supervision would form one economic entity with Central SASAC and affiliated companies'.[20] This conclusion led the commentators to argue that the Commission will be unlikely to consider the Central SASAC and regional SASACs and the SOEs under their control as belonging to the single economic entity.[21] Nevertheless, the Commission still examined the overlaps between Elkem and all other Chinese SOEs, including those operating under the supervision of the regional SASACs.[22] Although there were more than 200 Chinese companies active on the relevant markets, the merging parties have produced detailed ownership information in relation to the 40 largest companies, which constituted a significant part of the Chinese input on the respective markets.[23]

The *Bluestar/Elkem* case has clarified the Commission's approach toward assessment of the Chinese SOE governance under the EUMR, which was

---

18 Ibid., para 22.
19 Ibid., paras 24–28. See also Odd Stemsrud, '"China Inc" under Merger Regulation Review: the Commission's Approach to Acquisitions by Chinese Public Undertakings' (2011) 32 *European Competition Law Review* 481, 484.
20 Ibid., para 31.
21 See Jochem de Kok, 'Chinese SOEs under EU Competition Law' (2017) 40 *World Competition Law and Economics Review* 583, 604.
22 *China National Bluestar/Elkem*, paras 124–134.
23 Ibid., footnote 14.

further developed in the subsequent merger cases involving Chinese SOEs. First, the Commission specified that its assessment of the state control over the SOEs will be based on ascertaining the existence of the possibility to influence the SOE operations and the likelihood that such influence will be used in practice. Second, without reaching a definitive conclusion on whether SOEs controlled by the Central SASAC and those under supervision of regional SASACs constitute a single economic unit, the Commission conducted a 'worst case scenario' assessment assuming that all Chinese SOEs would act in a coordinated manner.

Within less than two months from the *Bluestar/Elkem* clearance decision, the Commission approved the establishment of the joint venture of PetroChina, a subsidiary of China National Petroleum Corporation (CNPC) and Ineos AG (Switzerland) for the operation of two petroleum refineries in Grangemouth (United Kingdom) and Lavera (France).[24] The 'Community dimension' under the EUMR was established on the basis of the worldwide turnover of CNPC Group, without considering other Chinese national oil companies (NOCs).[25] The relevant product markets included (1) production and sale of crude oil; (2) trading of crude oil and refined petroleum products; (3) ex-refinery sales of refined fuel products; (4) non-retail sales of refined fuel products; and (5) sale of other refined (non-fuel) products.[26] Besides CNPC, other Chinese NOCs, such as Sinopec and the China National Offshore Oil Corporation (CNOOC), were also active on these markets. Because the combined market shares of the Chinese NOCs did not exceed 25% on the relevant markets, the Commission did not consider it necessary to

> conclude on whether CNPC group should be qualified as a State-owned company within the meaning of the Merger Regulation and therefore whether all the other Chinese State owned undertakings active on the same sector should be considered as belonging to one economic entity.[27]

Another SOE-related merger case examined by the Commission in 2011 concerned a joint venture between Koninklijke DSM N.V. (Netherlands) and Sinochem Group, a Chinese SOE under the control of the Central

---

24 *PetroChina/Ineos/JV* (Case No. COMP/M.6151) [2011] OJ C216/18, decision of 13 May 2011.
25 Ibid., para 20.
26 Ibid., paras 23–29.
27 Ibid., para 31. See also Alexandr Svetlicinii, 'The Acquisitions of the Chinese State-Owned Enterprises under the EU Merger Control: Time for Reflection?' (2017) 67 *Revue Lamy de la concurrence* 30, 33.

SASAC.[28] The merging parties have argued that the SASAC performs the responsibilities of investor without interfering with production and operation activities of the SOEs.[29] Nevertheless, referring to the public information available at the SASAC's website, the Commission noted that the 'SASAC does in practice have certain powers to involve itself in Sinochem's commercial behaviour in a strategic manner, among others the right to approve mergers or of strategic investment decisions'.[30] The following excerpt from the Sinochem's annual report made the Commission to notice close cooperation between the SOE and the Chinese government: 'as the key state-owned enterprise, Sinochem Group is dedicated to serving the greater good of the national political stability, economic development, and social progress'.[31]

It should be noted that the aforementioned evidence in the form of general statements made by the SASAC and Sinochem led the Commission to the conclusion that the Chinese State's 'influence may be exercised through formal channels such as the SASAC, but also in less formal ways'[32] without any assessment on whether such influence was de facto exercised in the past or the likelihood that such influence will be exercised in the future. Following the pattern of assessment set in *Bluestar/Elkem*, the Commission opted for an open-ended assessment instead of making any definitive determination based on the aforementioned evidence. Similarly, the Commission considered a 'worst case scenario' where Sinochem would take part in a single economic entity with other Chinese SOEs. Although it has increased the market share of the merging parties on the relevant market, the anti-competitive effects would still be unlikely.[33]

ChemChina, a wholly owned Chinese SOE, again appeared under EUMR scrutiny when its subsidiary China National Agrochemical Corporation (CNAC) and Koor Industries notified acquisition of joint control over Makhteshim Agan Industries Ltd. (MAI).[34] Without any substantive

---

28 *DSM/Sinochem/JV* (Case No. COMP/M.6113) [2011] OJ C177/1, decision of 19 May 2011. See also Porter Elliott, 'The EU Commission Clears a Joint Venture in the Pharmaceutical Sector After Examining Possible Coordination Between Chinese State-Owned Companies (*Sinochem / DSM*)' (2011) *e-Competitions Bulletin* May 2011, Art. N° 41113 <www.concurrences.com/en/bulletin/news-issues/may-2011/the-eu-commission-clears-a-joint-venture-in-the-pharmaceutical-sector-after> accessed 31 July 2020.

29 Ibid., para 14.

30 Ibid., para 15.

31 Ibid.

32 Ibid.

33 Ibid., para 35.

34 *CNAC/Koor Industries/Makhteshim Agan Industries* (Case No. COMP/M.6141) [2011] OJ C309/1, decision of 3 October 2011.

assessment concerning ChemChina's independence from the SASAC or its relationship with other Chinese SOEs, the Commission moved its assessment to a 'worst case scenario' where all Chinese SOEs active on the relevant market were regarded as a single economic entity. Several respondents to the Commission's inquiry voiced their concerns that 'in the longer term the transaction might allow the merged entity to market and distribute its portfolio of active ingredients and possibly that of other Chinese SOEs more successfully in the EEA given MAI's presence in the EU and even to engage in predatory practices'.[35] Nevertheless, given insufficient market power of Chinese SOEs on the relevant markets and absence of the significant market barriers, the Commission considered the predatory pricing strategy unlikely. It noted that 'for a predatory practice to work, the merged entity would need to have enough market power so that it can reasonably expect to be able to raise prices once it has driven its rivals out of the market'.[36]

Another anti-competitive concern raised by the third parties was the possibility of horizontal collusion under the umbrella of the China Crop Protection Industry Association (CCPIA), bringing together Chinese SOEs, Chinese privately owned companies, and some foreign producers such as Syngenta.[37] It was alleged that the CCPIA could facilitate price increases and output restrictions for the benefit of its members. The Commission, however, noted that 'should Chinese agrochemical consortia limit output or fix prices or organize a foreclosure strategy on worldwide markets for certain active ingredients, this practice could fall under the antitrust rules of the Treaty on the Functioning of the European Union' and the companies thus had an incentive not to engage in such conduct.[38] The Commission noted among others that 'for such a strategy to be successful, other companies than just Chinese SOEs would need to participate given the limited market shares of Chinese SOEs in the active ingredients that are produced by either MAI or ChemChina/CNAC'.[39]

Following the string of merger cases cleared by the Commission in 2011, the commentators concluded that 'the European Commission has developed a well-defined practice in reviewing concentrations in which Chinese SOEs are involved'.[40] The flexible 'wait and see' approach to the

35 Ibid., para 61.
36 Ibid., para 62.
37 Ibid., para 77.
38 Ibid., para 78.
39 Ibid., para 81.
40 Kyriakos Fountoukakos and Camille Puech-Baron, 'The EU Merger Regulation and Transactions Involving States or State-Owned Enterprises: Applying Rules Designed for The

determination of the 'single economic unit' in these cases has been defended on the ground that

> if the Commission had found in one instance that the Chinese SOEs at hand belong or did not belong to a wider economic unit involving all companies active in the same markets and reporting to the Central SASAC, it would be very difficult for it to reach a different conclusion in a later decision.[41]

The Commission continued applying its 'wait and see' approach in the subsequent merger case involving China National Tyre & Rubber Co. Ltd. (CNRC), a wholly owned subsidiary of ChemChina, which notified its acquisition of Pirelli & C S.p.A., the renowned Italian tire manufacturer.[42] The aggregate turnover of ChemChina and Pirelli alone was sufficient to establish the 'Community dimension' under the EUMR. The Commission's assessment focused on whether decision-making power belonged to ChemChina or the Chinese government represented by the Central SASAC. CNRC referred to the Central SASAC as 'an executor of ownership' and as a 'non-managerial trustee'.[43] When applying the EU Commission's criteria for determining the independence of an undertaking, the notifying party argued that there are no interlocking directorships and that the Central SASAC does not require the SOEs to submit any commercially sensitive information.[44]

Without reaching a definitive conclusion on the independence of ChemChina from the Central SASAC, the Commission has considered possible horizontal and vertical overlaps of other Chinese SOEs with the commercial activities of the merging parties. Although several SOEs, such as China South Industries Group Corporation, the FAW Group, and the Dongfeng Motor Corporation, were vertically linked to the merging parties through the purchase of the automobile tires, the combined market share of CNRC and Pirelli did not raise anti-competitive concerns.[45] It was also noted that the merging parties were sourcing the rubber for the tires from

---

EU to The People's Republic of China' (2012) *Concurrences* N° 1–2012, Art. N° 41905 <www.concurrences.com/en/review/issues/no-1-2012/articles-en/The-EU-merger-regula tion-and> accessed 31 July 2020, 51.

41 Ibid., 52.

42 *CNRC/Pirelli* (Case No. COMP/M.7643) [2015] OJ C233/2, decision of 1 July 2015. See also Svetlicinii, 'The Acquisitions of the Chinese State-Owned Enterprises under the EU Merger Control: Time for Reflection?', 34.

43 Ibid., para 11.

44 Ibid., para 12.

45 Ibid., para 15.

other Chinese SOEs, such as CNPC, the China Petroleum and Chemical Corporation (Sinopec), CNOOC and Sinochem.[46] However, given that their combined share of the global market for rubber was below 10%, the Commission concluded that there were no grounds for input or customer foreclosure scenarios.[47] The Commission reached a similar conclusion in another merger case involving Sinopec:

> [s]ince neither at EEA nor at global level would the proposed transaction give rise to affected markets, even when considering the activities of the other Chinese SOEs, it is unlikely that competition concerns would arise as a result of the horizontal overlap between Mercuria and Sinopec's activities.[48]

The Commission's approach toward SOEs under control of the Central SASAC has been repeated in the cases concerning SOEs under supervision of the regional SASACs. For example, in the *Bright Food/Invermik* case, the Commission examined an acquisition by Bright Food Group, an SOE controlled by the Shanghai SASAC.[49] According to the Commission,

> the relationship between the Shanghai SASAC, which owns the Bright Food Group, and other similar, regional or central, government bodies will arise if the Bright Food Group is not considered an independent economic entity but part of an entity encompassing (at least) the Shanghai SASAC and all its controlled possessions.[50]

Naturally, the acquiring company argued that it has full decisional autonomy from the Shanghai SASAC and that 'the Shanghai SASAC is integrated in the Shanghai municipal government and acts primarily in its own interest, not in the interest of the central government'.[51] Although the merging parties have provided 'market information that includes all companies controlled by the central and regional SASACs, including but not limited to the Shanghai SASAC', the Commission did not make any determinations as to the ultimate control over the acquiring SOE.[52]

---

46 Ibid., para 16.
47 Ibid., para 18.
48 *Mercuria Energy Asset Management/Sinomart KTS Development/Vesta Terminals* (Case No. COMP/M.6807) [2013] OJ C37/35, decision of 7 March 2013, para 33.
49 *Bright Food Group/Invermik* (Case No. COMP/M.7709) [2015] OJ C348/1, decision of 14 September 2015.
50 Ibid., para 10.
51 Ibid., para 12.
52 Ibid., para 13.

3.3 Setting the precedent: the *EDF/CGN/NNB* decision

> *The CGN decision is the first decision involving a Chinese SOE in which the Commission has taken a firm stance on jurisdiction and abandoned, although to a limited extent, its 'wait and see' approach.*[53]

In 2016, the Commission examined a concentration whereby the French SOE Electricité de France S.A. (EDF) and the Chinese SOE China General Nuclear Power Corporation (CGN) sought to acquire joint control over NNB companies, which operated three nuclear power plants in the United Kingdom: Hinkley Point, Sizewell, and Bradwell.[54] At the time of notification, CGN was controlled by the Central SASAC (90% of shares), while the minority shareholding (10%) was held by the Guangdong SASAC.

According to CGN, it enjoyed operational independence from the Central SASAC due to the following circumstances: (1) the SOE law in China proclaimed separation of ownership from control; (2) the Central SASAC can appoint or remove CGN's management but cannot interfere with the day-to-day operations of the SOE; (3) CGN does not have any interlocking directorships with the SASAC.[55] The Commission, in its assessment, has referred to other provisions of China's SOE law and SASAC's regulations, which authorized the SASAC to supervise the investment decision making of the SOEs.[56] The SASAC's powers to appoint/remove senior management and to approve the investment plans of the SOE allowed the Commission to conclude that 'Central SASAC participates in major decision making, in the selection and supervision of senior management of SOEs and can interfere with strategic investment decisions'.[57] According to the Commission, the ability of the Central SASAC to coordinate the activities of the SOEs under its control was evidenced by the fact that in 2014 several centrally owned SOEs formed the China Nuclear Industry Alliance (CNIA).[58] With reference to the report of the World Nuclear Association, the Commission noted that the establishment of the CNIA was 'directed

---

53 Kyriakos Fountoukakos and Camille Puech-Baron, 'China/EU: The Gradual Evolution of the EU Commission's Merger Control Decisional Practice Towards SOEs Amidst an Increasingly Protectionist World' (2017) *Concurrences* N° 4–2017, Art. N° 84891 <www.concurrences.com/en/review/issues/no-4-2017/international/kyriakos-fountoukakos> accessed 31 July 2020, 5.

54 *EDF/CGN/NNB Group of Companies* (Case No. COMP/M.7850) [2016] OJ C151/1, decision of 10 March 2016.

55 Ibid., paras 34–36.

56 Ibid., para 39.

57 Ibid., para 42.

58 Ibid., para 44.

by the [Chinese] government to achieve some synergy' and is 'designed to eliminate detrimental or unseemly competition in export markets'.[59]

The ultimate conclusion reached by the Commission in the present case was as follows:

> [i]n view of the fact that Central SASAC can interfere with strategic investment decisions and can impose or facilitate coordination between SOEs at least with regard to SOEs active in the energy industry, the Commission concludes in the case at hand that CGN and other Chinese SOEs in that industry should not be deemed to have an independent power of decision from Central SASAC.[60]

Such an assessment prompted the comment that 'the Commission satisfied itself with the analysis of formal legal documents and with the fact of possibility or capacity that they give to Central SASAC to control and coordinate'.[61] At the same time, this broad determination of the 'single economic unit' encompassing all Chinese SOEs in the energy sector 'could have far-reaching implications, for example that mergers among, or restrictive agreements between Chinese SOEs within the same economic entity would not be subject to EU competition law'.[62] The references to the strategic importance of the nuclear energy industry and the SASAC's power to coordinate the business activities of the SOEs in that particular sector made some commentators doubt whether the Commission's approach in *EDF/CGN/NNB* would extend to all Chinese SOEs.[63] However, the Commission's reference to the wording of the Chinese legislation governing the ownership and control over SOEs without conducting an assessment on whether the SASAC's powers to influence the major business decisions of the SOEs have been exercised in practice, led others to suggest that 'the Commission's reasoning can be applied virtually directly to any other SOEs held by the Central SASAC'.[64] The presumption that SOEs lack

---

59 Ibid.

60 Ibid., para 49.

61 Václav Šmejkal, 'Chinese State-Owned Enterprises and the Concept of Undertaking under EU Competition Law' (2019) 6 *InterEULawEast* 31, 37.

62 Adrian Emch, 'EU Merger Control Complications for Chinese SOE Transactions' (Kluwer Competition Law Blog, 27 May 2016) <http://competitionlawblog.kluwercompetitionlaw. com/2016/05/27/eu-merger-control-complications-for-chinese-soe-transactions/?doing_wp_cron=1594978654.5616049766540527343750> accessed 31 July 2020.

63 See Tanisha A. James and M. Howard Morse, 'Regulatory Hurdles Facing Mergers with Chinese State-Owned Enterprises in the United States and the European Union' (2017) 1 *China Antitrust Law Journal* 1, 22.

64 de Kok, 'Chinese SOEs under EU Competition Law', 597.

autonomous decision-making power would automatically translate into the presumption that by having the controlling power over multiple SOEs, the SASAC can coordinate their commercial conduct. The burden of proof as to the absence of coordination by SASAC would shift to the SOEs, which would have to adduce evidence similar to that presented in the *EDF/Segebel* case.[65] The opponents of this interpretation have argued that the Commission did not set any presumption but continued its previous practice of case-by-case assessment considering the same criteria as in previous cases involving SOEs from the EEA and non-EEA jurisdictions: (1) the involvement of the State, directly or indirectly, in decisions concerning commercial activities; (2) the existence of formal or informal links between the SOEs; (3) the evidence of past coordination among the SOEs.[66]

The Commission's determination of the 'single economic unit' in the *EDF/CGN/NNB* case allowed it to combine the annual turnovers of two SOEs in the energy industry – CGN and ChemChina – in order to reach the 'Community dimension' under the EUMR. However, when addressing the potential anti-competitive effects of the concentration, the Commission noted that

> the question as to which companies shall be considered in the competitive assessment (i.e. CGN, Chinese SOEs controlled by Central SASAC and/or Chinese SOEs controlled by Local SASACs) can be left open, as the Transaction does not lead to competition concerns irrespective of the assessment of this point.[67]

This led the commentators to suggest that the Commission's determination of the 'single economic unit' in the present case was done solely for the purpose of establishing its jurisdiction to review a merger, which otherwise (due to the low EU-wide turnover of CGN) would not reach the 'Community dimension'.[68]

This observation is not without merit, given that the *EDF/CGN/NNB* decision comes after the 2015 merger of two Chinese SOEs in the railway

---

65 See *EDF/Segebel* (Case No. COMP/M.5549) [2009] OJ C57/9, decision of 12 November 2009.

66 See Geneviève Lallemand-Kirche, Caroline Tixier and Henri Piffaut, 'The Treatment of State-owned Enterprises in EU Competition Law: New Developments and Future Challenges' (2017) 8 *Journal of European Competition Law and Practice* 295, 305.

67 *EDF/CGN/NNB Group of Companies*, footnote 43.

68 See Fountoukakos and Puech-Baron, 'China/EU: The Gradual Evolution of The EU Commission's Merger Control Decisional Practice Towards SOEs Amidst an Increasingly Protectionist World', 5.

industry (China CNR Corporation Limited (CNR) and CSR Corporation Limited (CSR)), which created the world's largest train manufacturer – CRRC. On that occasion, the European MP Reinhard Bütikofer asked the Commission: '[w]hy did the Commission approve the merger of these two Chinese rail manufacturers, given the magnitude of the merger and the state support the company enjoys?'[69] Commissioner Vestager replied that the 'Commission did not have jurisdiction over the merger between the Chinese train builders CNR Corporation and CSR Corporation, given that the companies did not meet the relevant EU turnover thresholds'.[70]

The Commission's decision in the *EDF/CGN/NNB* was regarded as 'a milestone in correctly defining the scope of the relevant group in the case of Chinese SOEs'.[71] It establishes a precedent that would be certainly relevant to the Chinese SOEs operating in the energy markets and the nuclear sector in particular. At the same time, the decision left open the issue whether the SOEs under the control of the Central SASAC and the regional SASACs should be considered as members of the 'single economic entity' and whether the Commission's approach will be replicated in the cases involving SOEs from other sectors or industries. For instance, if the Chinese SOEs in the railway sector would be regarded as a single economic entity, the Commission would be precluded from the review of the aforementioned *CNR/CSR* merger, as the transaction would be regarded as an internal restructuring under the EUMR. This SOE-to-SOE concentration has been cleared by the competition authorities in China, Germany, and Singapore, all treating the Chinese railway manufacturers as previously independent undertakings for the purpose of merger assessment. For instance, under the Singapore Competition Act, a merger occurs 'when two or more independent undertakings amalgamate into a new undertaking and cease to exist as separate legal entities'.[72] Although both companies were under supervision of the Central SASAC, the merging parties argued that for the purposes of the Competition Act they were not 'under control' of the same entity due to the following reasons: (1) CNR and SCR have independent power of decision from the SASAC and the state intervention in the industry is minimal; (2) SASAC does not interfere with strategic decision making, production of

69 European Parliament, question for written answer E-002040–16 (8 March 2016) <www.europarl.europa.eu/doceo/document/E-8-2016-002040_EN.html> accessed 31 July 2020.
70 European Parliament, answer given by Ms Vestager on behalf of the Commission (3 June 2016) <www.europarl.europa.eu/doceo/document/E-8-2016-002040-ASW_EN.pdf> accessed 31 July 2020.
71 Alan Riley, 'Nuking Misconceptions: Hinkley Point, Chinese SOEs and EU Merger Law' (2016) 37 *European Competition Law Review* 301, 312.
72 Competition Act 46/2004 (Chapter 50B), Section 54(2).

operation activities; (3) both companies were listed on Shanghai and Hong Kong stock exchanges, which required them to have independent directors as members of the board.[73] The Competition Commission of Singapore accepted the preceding explanations and concluded that the transaction constitutes a merger within the meaning of the Competition Act.[74]

The expectations that the Commission will follow its more resolute stance on determination of the 'single economic unit' in cases involving Chinese SOEs in the aftermath of the *EDF/CGN/NNB* case have not been realized. In 2016, another subsidiary of ChemChina, China National Chemical Equipment Co., Ltd. (CNCE), notified its acquisition of Krauss-Maffei Group GmbH (Germany).[75] The acquiring company submitted that ChemChina has its own independent power of decision and does not form part of a single economic entity with other SOEs controlled by the Central SASAC or regional SASACs (provincial and municipal).[76] The decision does not contain any further arguments of the merging parties substantiating the aforementioned claim of ChemChina's independence from the SASAC. The Commission's assessment of this claim is also missing. Nevertheless, CNCE provided information about centrally owned (Aviation Industry Corporation of China, China National Petroleum Corporation, China Petroleum and Chemical Corporation) and regional SOEs (Dalian Rubber and Plastics Machinery, Qingdao Double Star) that were active on the relevant markets.[77] Given the low market shares of the merging parties, the question concerning operational independence of ChemChina has been left open.

In 2017, the Commission assessed the acquisition of Swiss agrochemical company Syngenta by ChemChina.[78] So far, it is the only merger case involving a Chinese SOE that was assessed following an in-depth investigation and concluded with the issuance of a conditional clearance

73 Competition Commission of Singapore (CCS), Case 400/001/15, Grounds of Decision in relation to the application for decision of the proposed merger between China CNR Corporation Limited and CSR Corporation Limited pursuant to section 57 of the Competition Act (17 February 2015), para 23.

74 Ibid., para 25.

75 *CNCE/KM Group* (Case No. COMP/M.7911) [2016] OJ C131/2, decision of 15 March 2016.

76 Ibid., para 7.

77 Ibid., para 10.

78 *ChemChina/Syngenta* (Case No. COMP/M.7962) [2017] OJ C186/8, decision of 5 April 2017. See also Jean-Christophe Mauger and others, 'The EU Commission Approves the Acquisition of Leading Global R&D Crop Protection Company by a Leading Global Generic Crop Protection Company, Subject to Remedies (*Chemchina / Syngenta*)' (2017) *e-Competitions Bulletin* April 2017, Art. N° 86504 <www.concurrences.com/en/bulletin/news-issues/april-2017/the-eu-commission-approves-acquisition-of-leading-global-r-d-crop-protection> accessed 31 July 2020.

decision under Article 8(2) EUMR. The Commission identified 17 Chinese SOEs at the central, regional, and municipal levels engaged in the production of the crop treatment products overlapping with those produced by Syngenta.[79] The merging parties adduced the following evidence in support of their claim that ChemChina is independent from the Central SASAC and cannot be included in the single economic unit together with the identified SOEs: (1) the SASAC follows the principle of separation between ownership and control and does not interfere with commercial decision making of the enterprises under its control; (2) the Central SASAC does not enjoy shareholder rights that would go beyond those offered for the protection of minority shareholders; (3) the Central SASAC does not exercise 'decisive influence' over ChemChina in relation to its budget, business plan, and commercial strategies; (4) the anti-monopoly legislation prohibits coordination among the competing companies, including the SOEs.[80] The merging parties have argued in particular that the 'Central SASAC's supervision over ChemChina is essentially limited by Chinese law to protecting the value of the State's assets'.[81]

The Commission once again decided to 'leave the nature of the link between the Central SASAC/other SoEs and ChemChina open and consider the most restrictive approach under which ChemChina is regarded as one economic entity with other companies owned by the Chinese Central Government'.[82] This distinction between the SOEs controlled by the Central SASAC and those under the supervision of the regional SASACs led the commentators to suggest that 'regionally and locally owned SOEs are not considered to form part of the same economic entity'.[83] This approach has been replicated in the *Weichai/Kion* merger in 2017, when the Commission examined an acquisition by Weichai Power Co. Ltd., a subsidiary of Shandong Heavy Industry Group Co. Ltd. (SHIG), a company controlled by the Shandong SASAC and Shandong Council for Social Security Fund.[84] When determining the entity with the ultimate power of decision, the Commission considered only Weichai, SHIG and the regional SASAC without reference to any other Chinese SOEs under the control of the Central SASAC or regional SASACs.[85] For procedural reasons the determination of a broader

---

79 Ibid., para 80.
80 Ibid., paras 84–87.
81 Ibid., para 86.
82 Ibid., para 88.
83 de Kok, 'Chinese SOEs under EU Competition Law', 605.
84 *Weichai/Kion* (Case No. COMP/M.8190) [2017] OJ C189/29, decision of 15 February 2017. See also *Weichai Power/Kion Group* (Case No. COMP/M.7169) [2014] OJ C240/11, decision of 15 July 2014.
85 Ibid., footnote 5.

'single economic unit' was not necessary – Weichai's EU-wide turnover exceeded EUR 250 million and thus reached the 'Community dimension' under the EUMR.[86] The Commission's assessment of the *ChemChina/ Syngenta* merger and the subsequent mergers involving Chinese SOEs demonstrates that '"wait and see" flexible approach therefore remains the Commission's preferred approach, even post-*CGN*, wherever possible'.[87]

3.4 Competitive assessment of mergers involving state owned enterprises: problems and possible ways forward

> *From central SASAC control over the central government-controlled SOEs, to local SASAC control of local SOEs, to state investment funds, to Party control of SOEs, their funders and regulators, the Middle Kingdom in these respects is a universe which is barely understood by western regulators.*[88]

The Commission's merger review practice under the EUMR reflected a cautious approach toward identifying a 'single economic unit' in cases involving Chinese SOEs (Annex II). With the notable exception of the *EDF/CGN/NNB* case, the Commission opted for a 'worst case scenario' assessment instead of reaching a definitive conclusion concerning the independence of the SOEs from the Central SASAC and regional SASACs. The analysts have repeatedly warned that the Commission's approach 'has created huge legal uncertainty and imposed heavy financial costs on transactions involving Chinese SOEs'.[89] This uncertainty can be described as a Catch-22 situation. If a centrally controlled SOE acquires a European company, the obligation to notify it to the Commission under the EUMR rules will depend on how the turnover thresholds will be calculated. Under the 'worst case scenario' where all SOEs under the control of the Central SASAC are regarded as a single economic unit, such transaction will be most likely subject to notification because the 'Community dimension' thresholds will be reached. By failing to notify, the SOE will become a target of hefty fines for non-compliance with the merger control regime.[90]

---

86 Ibid., para 11.
87 Fountoukakos and Puech-Baron, 'China/EU: The Gradual Evolution of The EU Commission's Merger Control Decisional Practice Towards SOEs Amidst an Increasingly Protectionist World', 7.
88 Riley, 'Nuking Misconceptions: Hinkley Point, Chinese SOEs and EU Merger Law', 324.
89 Ming Du, 'When China's National Champions Go Global: Nothing to Fear but Fear Itself?' (2014) 48 *Journal of World Trade* 1127, 1150.
90 EUMR, Article 14(2) authorizes the Commission to impose fines not exceeding 10% of the aggregate turnover on undertakings who failed to notify a concentration.

By notifying such concentration, the SOE may prejudice its own argument that it enjoys an independent power of decision that is not influenced by the Central SASAC.[91] It was suggested that the Commission's cautious and open-ended approach to defining the relevant 'single economic unit' would lead to a situation where 'all acquisitions by Chinese SOEs of a European business should be discussed with the Commission provided that the target meets the minimum requirements of the Merger Regulation'.[92] Additionally, if the 'worst case scenario' will be continuously applied by the Commission, this argument can be also employed by those who favor the consolidation of the 'European champions' as exemplified by the *Siemens/Alstom* merger attempt.[93] In other words,

> one can always argue that there is a huge Chinese single economic unit if not yet present in the EU, then surely at the horizon, and in a long-term perspective it poses a strong competitive pressure on all its EU-based rivals.[94]

Although not reaching a definitive conclusion concerning the scope of the single economic unit in mergers involving Chinese SOEs, the Commission has nevertheless engaged in a substantive assessment of their corporate governance and the ways the Chinese State exercises its ownership rights. In that assessment the Commission engaged in shifting between the analysis of the Chinese State's capacity of exercising a decisive influence over the SOE decisions and whether such influence was exercised in practice. For example, the Commission's analysis in *Bluestar/Elkem* and *DSM/Sinopec* suggests that the possibility of control is sufficient even though there was no clear evidence of interference by the SASAC or coordination of the SOEs' market behavior.[95] Zhang noted *inter alia* that

91 See Kiran Desai and Manu Mohan, 'Fear of the Chinese or Business as Usual at the European Commission? EU Merger Regulation and the Assessment of Transactions Involving Chinese State-Owned Enterprises' (CPI Antitrust Chronicle, 2011) <www.competitionpolicyinternational.com/fear-of-the-chinese-or-business-as-usual-at-the-european-commission-eu-merger-regulation-and-the-assessment-of-transactions-involving-chinese-state-owned-enterprises/> accessed 31 July 2020, 8–9.

92 Stemsrud, '"China Inc" under Merger Regulation Review: The Commission's Approach to Acquisitions by Chinese Public Undertakings', 485.

93 *Siemens/Alstom* (Case No. COMP/M.8677) [2019] OJ C300/12, decision of 6 February 2019.

94 Šmejkal, 'Chinese State-Owned Enterprises and the Concept of Undertaking under EU Competition Law', 39.

95 See Angela Huyue Zhang, 'The Single-Entity Theory: An Antitrust Time Bomb for Chinese State-Owned Enterprises' (2012) 8 *Journal of Competition Law & Economics* 805, 822–824.

contrary to the principle under the EUMR and previous Commission cases involving European SOEs, the Commission has seemed to focus on whether the Chinese State is able to exert influence over the SOEs, rather than whether such influence has been exerted in practice.[96]

In other cases, such as *EDF/CGN/NNB*, the Commission referred to evidence of the alleged past coordination by noting that the SASAC contributed to the establishment of the China Nuclear Industry Alliance and the joint promotion of the Hualong One nuclear technology by CGN and China National Nuclear Corporation, another SOE under supervision of the Central SASAC.[97]

The Commission's

decision practice illustrates that the Commission has often quickly jumped to the conclusion that an SOE does not have autonomy from the State on the basis of the State's ability to exert (decisive) influence, without having considered whether the State has actually exerted such influence in practice.[98]

In that regard, Zhang argued that in order to preserve the meaning and purpose of the recital 22 EUMR concerning the non-discrimination between SOEs and private companies, the determination of the 'single economic entity' should be based not on the *de jure* powers of the state to influence the conduct of an SOE but rather on the *de facto* exercise of this control: 'while the State in theory can influence its SOEs, if the SOEs in fact operate independently from each other, then a merger between them will deprive the market of two real competitors'.[99] By calling the Commission's approach 'anything but consistent', Zhang pointed out the differences in applying the principle of the recital 22 EUMR to cases involving European SOEs (*Neste/IVO*, *EDF/Segebel*) where the Commission analyzed *de facto* exercise of state control and those involving non-European SOEs (*Rosneft/TNK-BP*, *Bluestar/Elkem*) where *de jure* control has raised anti-competitive concerns.[100]

For better understanding of the Commission's approach toward identifying the 'single economic unit' in merger cases involving Chinese SOEs, one

96 Ibid., 830.
97 *EDF/CGN/NNB Group of Companies*, paras 44–48.
98 de Kok, 'Chinese SOEs under EU Competition Law', 612.
99 Angela Huyue Zhang, 'The Antitrust Paradox of China, Inc.' (2017) 50 *International Law and Politics* 159, 172.
100 Ibid., 180–188.

should distinguish between the procedural and the substantive role of this concept in the merger assessment. The procedural function, as discussed in Chapter 1 refers to the calculation of the relevant turnover in order to establish whether it reaches the requisite 'Community dimension'.[101] As specified in the Jurisdictional Notice, 'for the purposes of calculating turnover of State-owned undertakings, account is only taken of those undertakings which belong to the same economic unit, having the same independent power of decision'.[102] As a result, if 'a State-owned company is not subject to any coordination with other State-controlled holdings'[103] it will be treated as independent and the turnover of other SOEs owned by the same state will not be taken into account. From the cases examined in the present chapter, except for the *EDF/CGN/NNB* merger, the turnover of the acquiring SOE alone was sufficient for triggering notification obligation under the EUMR and the Commission did not have to identify a broader 'single economic unit' to assert jurisdiction for merger review.

When it comes to the substantive assessment of the notified concentrations, the identification of the 'single economic unit' should have important repercussions for the forecast of the merger's effect on competition, as the companies taking part in the relevant 'single economic unit' could engage in various forms of anti-competitive collusion. In that regard, the mere conclusion that the Chinese State has a possibility to exercise decisive influence over conduct of the SOEs under its ownership would hardly represent a sufficient evidence of the likelihood that certain anti-competitive practices would be realized in a post-merger environment. As a result, the assessment of the possible anti-competitive scenarios involving SOEs should require additional evidence, such as instances of past coordination facilitated by the state, the existence of the state policies that require coordination, or certain strategic behavior of its SOEs on the global markets.

The differentiated approach to the determination of the 'single economic unit' has been endorsed by the General Court, which acknowledged that the definition of single economic unit in the field of merger control may not be applicable in other fields:

> [a]s the present case is neither in the field of cartels nor in that of mergers, but in that of state aid, reference should be made to the concept of economic unit developed by case law in this field. In that regard, as has already been pointed out, the case law has granted the Commission a

---

101 EUMR, Article 1(2).
102 Jurisdictional Notice, para 193.
103 Ibid., para 194.

wide discretion in determining whether companies which are part of a group should be regarded as an economic unit.[104]

The European Court of Justice concurred: 'the concept of an economic unit in State aid matters can differ from that applicable in other areas of competition law'.[105] Several scholars, including Petit and Šmejkal,[106] highlight the differences between *ex ante* (merger control and state aid) and *ex post* (antitrust) assessment. Whereas *ex ante* assessment requires estimation of future developments, the application of the 'worst case scenario' approach should be acceptable and the SOEs could be regarded as members of the 'single economic unit'. In the *ex post* assessment of the anti-competitive practices involving SOEs, the application of Article 101 TFEU could lead to a different determination that would regard SOEs as independent undertakings that entered into an anti-competitive agreement. Based on the role of the CPC in the exercising control over SOEs and private companies alike, Petit suggested that for the purpose of merger control, all Chinese SOEs and private companies with CPC cells, as well as state owned banks, should be treated as a single economic entity regardless of the industry in which they operate.[107] For the *ex post* assessment under Article 101 TFEU, he suggested that 'antitrust cases involving Chinese firms should be investigated on the default assumption that there is an underlying coordination scheme among them'.[108]

At the same time, as indicated by the Commission's merger decisions involving Chinese SOEs, the determination of the 'single economic unit' for the purpose of estimating the likelihood of the anti-competitive scenario

104 Case T-303/05 *AceaElectrabel Produzione SpA v Commission* [2009] ECR 2009 II-00137, judgment of 8 September 2009, paras 138–139.
105 Case C-480/09 P *AceaElectrabel Produzione SpA v Commission* [2010] ECR I-13355, judgment of 16 December 2010, para 66. See also Martin Nettesheim, 'Obligation Imposed on a Newly Founded Company to Repay a Previous Unlawful Subsidy' (2011) 2 *Journal of European Competition Law and Practice* 557; Markus Wellinger, 'The EU Court of Justice Endorses the "Single Economic Unit" Reasoning of the Commission in a Decision Concerning State Aid Intended to Grant Reduction of Greenhouse Gas Emissions (*AceaElectrabel*)' (2010) e-*Competitions* December 2010, Art. N° 41267 <www. concurrences.com/en/bulletin/news-issues/december-2010/the-eu-court-of-justice-endorses-the-single-economic-unit-reasoning-of-the-en> accessed 31 July 2020.
106 See Nicolas Petit, 'Chinese State Capitalism and Western Antitrust Policy' (American Security Project, 22 June 2016) <www.americansecurityproject.org/featured-paper-chinese-state-capitalism-and-western-antitrust-policy/> accessed 31 July 2020; Šmejkal, 'Chinese State-Owned Enterprises and the Concept of Undertaking under EU Competition Law'.
107 Petit, 'Chinese State Capitalism and Western Antitrust Policy', 12.
108 Ibid., 16.

is not necessary. However, the Commission's assessment would be more credible if instead of referring to the 'worst case scenario', the likelihood of an anti-competitive post-merger scenario would be substantiated by a more thorough factual analysis. The examples of such analysis can be found in the Commission's anti-dumping investigations. For example, in 2018, the Commission imposed countervailing duties on automotive tires originating from China.[109] In particular, it investigated the products of the following Chinese companies, which accounted for more than 50% of the respective EU imports: China National Tire Group, Giti Group, Hankook Group, and Xingyuan Group.[110]

The Commission examined *inter alia* the Chinese State's involvement in the acquisition of Italian car tire manufacturer Pirelli by CNRC.[111] It established that the acquisition has been facilitated by the PRC government in the following ways: (1) a grant from the Central SASAC; (2) a preferential loan from a consortium of state owned banks; (3) a refund of the interest paid on the loan by the MOFCOM; (4) an equity participation by the Silk Road Fund (SRF); (5) an equity participation by China Cinda Asset Management Company Ltd. (Cinda).[112] The Commission assessed the exercise of the meaningful influence by the government over SRF and Cinda to determine whether they acted as 'public bodies' implementing state policies on foreign investment. The formal existence of control has been confirmed through the majority state shareholdings and the general statements such as Cinda's commitment to

> earnestly study and implement the spirit of the 19th National Congress of the CPC and Xi Jinping Thought on Socialism with Chinese Characteristics for a New Era, vigorously strengthen the overall leadership of the Party and provide strong political guarantee for the development of the Company.[113]

---

109 Commission Implementing Regulation (EU) 2018/1690 of 9 November 2018 imposing definitive countervailing duties on imports of certain pneumatic tyres, new or retreaded, of rubber, of a kind used for buses or lorries and with a load index exceeding 121 originating in the People's Republic of China and amending Commission Implementing Regulation (EU) 2018/1579 imposing a definitive anti-dumping duty and collecting definitively the provisional duty imposed on imports of certain pneumatic tyres, new or retreaded, of rubber, of a kind used for buses or lorries, with a load index exceeding 121 originating in the People's Republic of China and repealing Implementing Regulation (EU) 2018/163, C/1018/7349, OJ L283/1, 12 November 2018.
110 Ibid., para 35.
111 See *CNRC/Pirelli*.
112 Commission Implementing Regulation (EU) 2018/1690, paras 335–339.
113 Ibid., para 345.

The Commission has further investigated whether the state influence was exercised in practice. It has noted the 13th Five-Year Plan for the Development of Foreign Trade and the 2015 Guiding Opinions on promotion of international production capacity issued by the State Council,[114] which were qualified by the PRC government as non-binding.[115] These policy documents instructed the SOEs to 'go global' by means of mergers, acquisitions, investments, and other forms of asserting presence on the global markets. The Commission concluded that these documents established 'a normative framework that had to be adhered to by the managers and supervisors appointed by the [government] and accountable to the [government]'.[116] On that basis, the Commission was able to conclude that both SRF and Cinda acted as 'public bodies' within the meaning of the EU anti-dumping legislation.[117]

Although the Commission's anti-dumping investigations represent lengthy and thorough fact-finding exercises of the past events, the assessment of the Chinese State's influence on the market conduct of its SOEs could be also employed in the merger investigations under the EUMR, as long as they add to the credibility of the Commission's forecast of the anti-competitive post-merger scenarios involving Chinese SOEs. The preceding review of the merger cases involving Chinese SOEs under the EUMR demonstrates that following its established practice, when assessing the state control over the SOEs, the European Commission continuously focused on the ownership-related aspects of the Chinese SOEs' governance, exercised by the Central SASAC and the regional SASACs. This effectively left out the mechanism of political control over the SOEs and their management, as discussed in Chapter 2. To remedy this deficiency it was suggested that

> comprehensive analysis of Chinese SOEs necessitates, then, to adopt a two-level analysis of corporate governance: a legal one where the power is exercised by state's entity such as SASAC and an underlying political one where the [CPC] assumes an essential role.[118]

An opposite approach would create a discrimination between state owned and privately owned enterprises, both groups affected by the political

---

114 Guiding Opinions of the State Council on Promotion of International Production Capacity and Equipment Manufacturing Cooperation, No. 30/2015, 13 May 2015.
115 Commission Implementing Regulation (EU) 2018/1690, para 124.
116 Ibid., para 353.
117 Regulation (EU) 2016/1036 on protection against dumped imports from countries not members of the European Union, OJ L176/21, 30 June 2016.
118 Julien Briguet, 'The State's Invisible Hand: Chinese SOEs Facing EU Antitrust Law' (2018) 52 *Journal of World Trade* 839, 851.

control and benefiting from the special relationships with the Chinese State. This 'ownership bias' or 'ownership trap' currently present in the Commission's merger assessment under the EUMR does not account for the specifics of the political and institutional environment under which the Chinese SOEs operate. It also distorts the commitment to the competitive neutrality, which stands at the basis of the EUMR.

Although being focused primarily on the role and powers of the SASAC, the Commission's merger decisions contain accidental evidence of other, non-ownership channels, through which the Chinese State can exercise decisive influence on the market conduct of the SOEs under its control. For example, in the *DSM/Sinochem* case, the Commission acknowledged that state 'influence may be exercised through formal channels such as SASAC, but also in less formal ways'.[119] The continuous focus on the SASAC has left out other institutions through which the state control can guide the SOEs' decision making. For example, the Central SASAC is an entity established under the State Council, which also controls several SOEs directly (Annex I, Table 3). As discussed in Chapter 2, the appointments and evaluation of the management personnel in the SOEs is entrusted to the CPC organs, including the personnel departments and the supervisory commissions. These party institutions, in practice, could play an even greater role than the SASACs in ensuring the implementation of the state policies and guidelines by the SOEs. In that regard, Riley argues that all SOEs under the control of the Central SASAC should be regarded as single economic entity, whereas the CPC or Chinese party-state should be viewed as a 'person' under Article 3(1) EUMR.[120] Indeed, the Jurisdictional Notice clarified that the term 'person controlling another undertaking' extends to public bodies[121] and the Commission's merger control practice encountered the instances where the whole State[122] or a public institution[123] were regarded as controlling person. By conducting a more thorough investigation into the exercise of state control over its SOEs, the Commission will be also expected to clarify the distinction between the situation where the Chinese State is acting as a shareholder from that where it exercises its prerogatives as a public authority,

> in so far as they are limited to the protection of the public interest, do not constitute control within the meaning of the Merger Regulation to the

---

119 *DSM/Sinochem/JV*, para 15.
120 See Riley, 'Nuking Misconceptions: Hinkley Point, Chinese SOEs and EU Merger Law', 322.
121 Jurisdictional Notice, para 12.
122 See *Air France/Sabena* (Case IV/M.157) [1992] OJ C272/5, decision of 5 October 1992. In that case the Belgian State was viewed as a controlling person.
123 See *Kali und Salz/MDK/Treuhand* (Case IV/M.308) Commission Decision 94/449/EC [1993] OJ L186/38. In that case German public institution Treuhandanstalt was viewed as a controlling person.

extent that they have neither the aim nor the effect of enabling the State to exercise a decisive influence over the activity of the undertaking.[124]

In its merger control practice, the Commission has recognized this exception in cases concerning European SOEs, where the State had certain golden share or veto rights, the exercise of which was limited by the public interest considerations.[125]

It should be specified, however, that the consideration of corporate, political, and other channels of state control over the SOEs should be used not for the purpose of extending the notion of 'single economic unit' to eventually all Chinese SOEs. Such extension would cause a wave of notifications as the 'Community dimension' will be reached even by small SOE acquisitions and it would arguably exclude SOE-to-SOE mergers from the ambit of the EUMR. The assessment of the corporate, political, and other means of control should be used for a more thorough assessment of the likelihood of anti-competitive scenarios in order to produce well-grounded conclusions reviewable by the CJEU, especially in cases of prohibited or conditionally cleared concentrations. Such thorough assessment would also strengthen the Commission's reasoning in the clearance decisions, which up until now easily turned to a 'worst case scenario', as the low market shares of the Chinese SOEs on the global and European markets, even when considered together, did not lead to competition concerns.

Bibliography

Briguet J, 'The State's Invisible Hand: Chinese SOEs Facing EU Antitrust Law' (2018) 52 *Journal of World Trade* 839.

de Kok J, 'Chinese SOEs under EU Competition Law' (2017) 40 *World Competition Law and Economics Review* 583.

Depoortere F, 'The EU Commission Clears in Phase I a Merger in the Silicon Sector Examining Possible Coordination by the Chinese State of Market Behaviour of Chinese State-Owned Companies (China National Bluestar/Elkem)' (2011) *e-Competitions Bulletin* March 2011, Art. N° 38917 <www.concurrences.com/en/bulletin/news-issues/march-2011/The-EU-Commission-clears-in-phase> accessed 31 July 2020.

Desai K, M Mohan, 'Fear of the Chinese or Business as Usual at the European Commission? EU Merger Regulation and the Assessment of Transactions Involving Chinese State-Owned Enterprises' (CPI Antitrust Chronicle, 2011) <www.competition policyinternational.com/fear-of-the-chinese-or-business-as-usual-at-the-european-

---

124 Jurisdictional Notice, para 53.
125 See *Tractebel/Distrigaz II* (Case IV/M.493) [1994] OJ C249/3, decision of 1 September 1994, para 11. In that case the Commission referred to the ministerial veto power exercised by the Belgian State for the purposes of national sovereignty and energy policy.

commission-eu-merger-regulation-and-the-assessment-of-transactions-involving-chinese-state-owned-enterprises/> accessed 31 July 2020.

Du M, 'When China's National Champions Go Global: Nothing to Fear but Fear Itself?' (2014) 48 *Journal of World Trade* 1127.

Elliott P, 'The EU Commission Clears a Joint Venture in the Pharmaceutical Sector after Examining Possible Coordination Between Chinese State-Owned Companies (Sinochem/DSM)' (2011) *e-Competitions Bulletin* May 2011, Art. N° 41113 <www.concurrences.com/en/bulletin/news-issues/may-2011/the-eu-commission-clears-a-joint-venture-in-the-pharmaceutical-sector-after> accessed 31 July 2020.

Emch A, 'EU Merger Control Complications for Chinese SOE Transactions' (Kluwer Competition Law Blog, 27 May 2016) <http://competitionlawblog.kluwercompetitionlaw.com/2016/05/27/eu-merger-control-complications-for-chinese-soe-transactions/?doing_wp_cron=1594978654.5616049766540527343750> accessed 31 July 2020.

Fountoukakos K, C Puech-Baron, 'China/EU: The Gradual Evolution of the EU Commission's Merger Control Decisional Practice towards SOEs Amidst an Increasingly Protectionist World' (2017) *Concurrences N° 4–2017*, Art. N° 84891 <www.concurrences.com/en/review/issues/no-4-2017/international/kyriakos-fountoukakos> accessed 31 July 2020.

———, 'The EU Merger Regulation and Transactions Involving States or State-Owned Enterprises: Applying Rules Designed for the EU to the People's Republic of China' (2012) *Concurrences N° 1–2012*, Art. N° 41905 <www.concurrences.com/en/review/issues/no-1-2012/articles-en/The-EU-merger-regulation-and> accessed 31 July 2020.

James TA, MH Morse, 'Regulatory Hurdles Facing Mergers with Chinese State-Owned Enterprises in the United States and the European Union' (2017) 1 *China Antitrust Law Journal* 1.

Lallemand-Kirche G, C Tixier, H Piffaut, 'The Treatment of State-Owned Enterprises in EU Competition Law: New Developments and Future Challenges' (2017) 8 *Journal of European Competition Law and Practice* 295.

Mauger JC, others, 'The EU Commission Approves the Acquisition of Leading Global R&D Crop Protection Company by a Leading Global Generic Crop Protection Company, Subject to Remedies (Chemchina/Syngenta)' (2017) *e-Competitions Bulletin* April 2017, Art. N° 86504 <www.concurrences.com/en/bulletin/news-issues/april-2017/the-eu-commission-approves-acquisition-of-leading-global-r-d-crop-protection> accessed 31 July 2020.

Nettesheim M, 'Obligation Imposed on a Newly Founded Company to Repay a Previous Unlawful Subsidy' (2011) 2 *Journal of European Competition Law and Practice* 557.

Petit N, 'Chinese State Capitalism and Western Antitrust Policy' (American Security Project, 22 June 2016) <www.americansecurityproject.org/featured-paper-chinese-state-capitalism-and-western-antitrust-policy/> accessed 31 July 2020.

Riley A, 'Nuking Misconceptions: Hinkley Point, Chinese SOEs and EU Merger Law' (2016) 37 *European Competition Law Review* 301.

Šmejkal V, 'Chinese State-Owned Enterprises and the Concept of Undertaking under EU Competition Law' (2019) 6 *InterEULawEast* 31.

Stemsrud O, '"China Inc" under Merger Regulation Review: The Commission's Approach to Acquisitions by Chinese Public Undertakings' (2011) 32 *European Competition Law Review* 481.

Svetlicinii A, 'The Acquisitions of the Chinese State-Owned Enterprises under the EU Merger Control: Time for Reflection?' (2017) 67 *Revue Lamy de la concurrence* 30.

Wellinger M, 'The EU Court of Justice Endorses the "Single Economic Unit" Reasoning of the Commission in a Decision Concerning State Aid Intended to Grant Reduction of Greenhouse Gas Emissions (AceaElectrabel)' (2010) *e-Competitions* December 2010, Art. N° 41267 <www.concurrences.com/en/bulletin/news-issues/december-2010/the-eu-court-of-justice-endorses-the-single-economic-unit-reasoning-of-the-en> accessed 31 July 2020.

Zhang AH, 'The Antitrust Paradox of China, Inc.' (2017) 50 *International Law and Politics* 159.

Zhang AH, 'The Single-Entity Theory: An Antitrust Time Bomb for Chinese State-Owned Enterprises' (2012) 8 *Journal of Competition Law & Economics* 805.

European Commission (merger cases)

Air France/Sabena (Case IV/M.157) [1992] OJ C272/5.

AVIC/Pacific Century Motors (Case No. COMP/M.6142) [2011] OJ C94/2.

Bright Food Group/Invermik (Case No. COMP/M.7709) [2015] OJ C348/1.

Cathay Pacific Airways/Air China/ACC (Case No. COMP/M.5841) [2010] OJ C208/3.

ChemChina/Syngenta (Case No. COMP/M.7962) [2017] OJ C186/8.

China National Bluestar/Elkem (Case No. COMP/M.6082) [2011] OJ C274/7.

CNAC/Koor Industries/Makhteshim Agan Industries (Case No. COMP/M.6141) [2011] OJ C309/1.

CNCE/KM Group (Case No. COMP/M.7911) [2016] OJ C131/2.

CNRC/Pirelli (Case No. COMP/M.7643) [2015] OJ C233/2.

COSCO Shipping/OOIL (Case No. COMP/M.8594) [2017] OJ C79/2.

DSM/Sinochem/JV (Case No. COMP/M.6113) [2011] OJ C177/1.

EDF/CGN/NNB Group of Companies (Case No. COMP/M.7850) [2016] OJ C151/1.

EDF/Segebel (Case No. COMP/M.5549) [2009] OJ C57/9.

Kali und Salz/MDK/Treuhand (Case IV/M.308) Commission Decision 94/449/EC [1993] OJ L186/38.

Mercuria Energy Asset Management/Sinomart KTS Development/Vesta Terminals (Case No. COMP/M.6807) [2013] OJ C37/35.

Neste/IVO (Case No. IV/M.931) [1998] OJ C218/4.

PetroChina/Ineos/JV (Case No. COMP/M.6151) [2011] OJ C216/18.

Republic of Austria/Hypo Group Alpe Adria (Case No. COMP/M.5861) [2010] OJ C236/1.

Siemens/Alstom (Case No. COMP/M.8677) [2019] OJ C300/12.

Soffin/Hypo Real Estate (Case No. COMP/M.5508) [2009] OJ C147/8.

Tractebel/Distrigaz II (Case IV/M.493) [1994] OJ C249/3.

Weichai/Kion (Case No. COMP/M.8190) [2017] OJ C189/29.

Weichai Power/Kion Group (Case No. COMP/M.7169) [2014] OJ C240/11.

4 From merger control to foreign investment screening in the European Union

4.1 Regulatory proposals for the reform of the EU merger control

I remain firmly convinced that EU merger control must remain anchored to its own rules and purposes at all times, irrespective of the nationality of the companies concerned.[1]

The difficulties of applying traditional merger control tests to the acquisitions of the Chinese SOEs, as demonstrated in Chapter 3, have stirred the discussion on the effectiveness of the current EU merger control regime when addressing possible anti-competitive distortions caused by such acquisitions. This discussion, led in both academic and policy circles, has produced a number of proposals for the reform of the EU merger control. This section examines the most notable of these proposals as well as the approach taken by the European Commission.

In 2017, the Ministerial Meeting of the Friends of Industry, which included the representatives of the 18 Member States, urged the Commission to address

> challenges that are raised by competitive foreign industries which are supported through tools that are not in accordance with their obligations under international law or the applicable principles of the EU internal market including EU competition law and find an appropriate and balanced response.[2]

---

1 Joaquín Almunia, Vice President of the European Commission responsible for Competition Policy, SPEECH/11/243 'Recent Developments and Future Priorities in EU Competition Policy', International Competition Law Forum, St. Gallen (8 April 2011) <https://ec.europa.eu/commission/presscorner/detail/en/SPEECH_11_243> accessed 31 July 2020.
2 Joint Declaration on Industrial Policy by Austria, Belgium, Bulgaria, Croatia, Czech Republic, France, Germany, Hungary, Italy, Latvia, Lithuania, Luxembourg, Malta, Netherlands, Poland, Portugal, Romania, Slovak Republic, Slovenia and Spain (30 June 2017) <www.

The inclusion of the industrial policy considerations into the EU competition policy was also supported by 18 Member States at the 2018 Ministerial Meeting of the Friends of Industry: '[w]hile the major powers do not hesitate to defend their national champions, Europe must take account, in its competition policy, the evolution of the global competitive environment in terms of investment, trade and industry'.[3]

The industrial policy proposals coming from the Member States have only intensified after the Commission's prohibition of the *Siemens/Alstom* merger in February 2019.[4] The Commission blocked the proposed merger because it 'would have resulted in higher prices for the signalling systems that keep passengers safe and for the next generations of very high-speed trains'.[5] The proposed merger had the strong backing of both French and German governments. As a result, the Commission's decision to block the transaction prompted further calls for the reform of the 'outdated' competition rules that 'hold us back' when compared with the Chinese SOE consolidations such as the one that produced CRRC, a global rail leader.[6]

---

bmwi.de/Redaktion/DE/Downloads/E/gemeinsame-erklaerung-friends-of-industry-en. pdf?__blob=publicationFile&v=10> accessed 31 July 2020, 5.

3 Joint Statement by France, Austria, Croatia, Czech Republic, Estonia, Finland, Germany, Greece, Hungary, Italy, Latvia, Luxembourg, Malta, Netherlands, Poland, Romania, Slovakia, Spain (18 December 2018) <www.bmwi.de/Redaktion/DE/Downloads/F/friends-of-industry-6th-ministerial-meeting-declaration.pdf?__blob=publicationFile&v=6> accessed 31 July 2020, 4.

4 *Siemens/Alstom* (Case No. COMP/M.8677) [2019] OJ C300/12, decision of 6 February 2019. See also David Henry and Jacques Buhart, 'The EU Commission Prohibits a Merger in the Railway Sector and Reaffirms that Industrial Policy Objectives Have No Role to Play When It Comes to Applying the EU Merger Control Rules *(Siemens / Alstom)*' (2019) *e-Competitions* February 2019, Art. N° 89282 <www.concurrences.com/en/bulletin/news-issues/february-2019/the-eu-commission-prohibits-a-merger-in-the-railway-sector-and-reaffirms-that> accessed 31 July 2020; Porter Elliott, 'The EU Commission Prohibits a Merger in the Market for Railway Signalling and Very High-Speed Trains *(Siemens / Alstom)*' (2019) *e-Competitions* February 2019, Art. N° 89603 <www.concurrences.com/en/bulletin/news-issues/february-2019/the-eu-commission-prohibits-a-merger-in-the-market-for-railway-signalling-and-89603> accessed 31 July 2020; Clara García Fernández, Miguel Troncoso Ferrer and Sara Moya Izquierdo, 'The EU Commission Prohibits a Merger in the Market for Railway Signalling and Very High-Speed Trains *(Siemens / Alstom)*' (2019) *e-Competitions* February 2019, Art. N° 89741 <www.concurrences.com/en/bulletin/news-issues/february-2019/the-eu-com mission-prohibits-a-merger-in-the-market-for-railway-signalling-and-en> accessed 31 July 2020; Thomas Oster, Florence Leroux and Jörg Witting, 'The EU Commission Prohibits a Merger in the Railway Sector *(Siemens / Alstom)*' (2019) *e-Competitions* February 2019, Art. N° 94671 <www.concurrences.com/en/bulletin/news-issues/february-2019/the-eu-commission-prohibits-a-merger-in-the-railway-sector-siemens-alstom> accessed 31 July 2020.

5 EU Commission, press release IP/19/881 'Mergers: Commission Prohibits Siemens' Proposed Acquisition of Alstom' (6 February 2019) <https://ec.europa.eu/commission/presscorner/detail/en/IP_19_881> accessed 31 July 2020.

6 Government of France, 'The European Commission's Decision on the Alstom-Siemens Merger Throws the Need to Revise Competition Law Into Sharp Focus' (8 February 2019)

The subsequently released 'Franco-German Manifesto for a European Industrial Policy Fit for the 21st Century' questioned whether the existing regulatory framework allows the European companies to compete effectively with the Chinese SOEs:

> When some countries heavily subsidize their own companies, how can companies operating mainly in Europe compete fairly? Of course, we must continue to argue for a fairer and more effective global level playing field, but in the meantime, we need to ensure our companies can actually grow and compete.[7]

In order to remedy the alleged competitive disadvantage encountered by the European companies, France and Germany put forward the following reform proposals: (1) reforming EU merger control rules in a way that would allow consideration of the state support received by the merging companies; (2) updating the current merger control guidelines to allow the Commission to consider competition on the global markets; (3) granting the Council of the EU the right to hear appeals against the Commission's merger decisions. Along similar lines goes the proposal 'to empower the EU's High Representative to invoke a security clause, which would then lead to a Commission college decision on whether to overrule the proposal from the Competition Commissioner'.[8]

The German Industrial Strategy 2030 also called for reforming the EU competition law: 'European and German competition law must be reviewed and changed where applicable so that international competition "at eye level" remains possible for German and European companies'.[9] This policy document addressed the issue of foreign investment restrictions: '[t]he state prohibition of company take-overs by foreign competitors must be based on strict requirements in future too and may only happen if this is necessary to defend against risks to national security, including the area of critical infrastructures'.[10]

<www.gouvernement.fr/en/the-european-commission-s-decision-on-the-alstom-siemens-merger-throws-the-need-to-revise> accessed 31 July 2020.

7 'A Franco-German Manifesto for a European Industrial Policy Fit for the 21st Century' (19 February 2019) <www.gouvernement.fr/en/a-franco-german-manifesto-for-a-european-industrial-policy-fit-for-the-21st-century> accessed 31 July 2020.

8 Mark Leonard and others, 'Redefining Europe's Economic Sovereignty' (European Council on Foreign Relations, 2019) <www.ecfr.eu/publications/summary/redefining_europes_economic_sovereignty> accessed 31 July 2020, 8.

9 Federal Ministry for Economic Affairs and Energy, 'National Industrial Strategy 2030: Strategic Guidelines for a German and European Industrial Policy' (5 February 2019) <www.bmwi.de/Redaktion/EN/Publikationen/Industry/national-industry-strategy-2030.html> accessed 31 July 2020, 14.

10 Ibid., 12.

On 4 July 2019, France, Germany, and Poland put forward a proposal on modernizing the EU competition policy: 'the state control of undertakings should be stringently taken into account when calculating turnover' and in the assessment of foreign SOE acquisitions 'the financial power of state-controlled and subsidized undertakings should adequately be taken into account'.[11] More specifically, 'particular attention should be paid to competition from third countries' state-backed or subsidized companies' because 'a low profitability of market entry may not be a significant barrier to entry for directly or indirectly subsidized third country companies that adopt a strategic approach'.[12] In November 2019, Industry4Europe coalition argued for a more aggressive deployment of the EU trade defense and foreign direct investment (FDI) screening instruments:

> [i]n the absence of international competition rules, a level playing field should be achieved through-efficient deployment of EU Trade Defence Instruments, as well as the recently adopted Foreign Direct Investment (FDI) screening mechanism, the agreement on the International Procurement Instrument (IPI) and better enforcement of EU rules.[13]

On 4 February 2020, a letter to Commissioner Vestager by France, Germany, Italy, and Poland called among others for 'modernization' of the Commission's guidelines on the assessment of horizontal mergers and on the definition of the relevant market. According to the authors, such modernization would make

> our competition toolbox more efficient and effective in tackling potential abusive behavior in the single market of economic operators from outside the EU, including state-backed or subsidized companies and this strengthening the competitiveness of EU industry and European value chains.[14]

---

11 Federal Ministry for Economic Affairs and Energy, 'Modernising EU Competition Policy' <www.bmwi.de/Redaktion/DE/Downloads/M-O/modernising-eu-competition-policy. pdf?__blob=publicationFile&v=4> accessed 31 July 2020, 1.

12 Ibid., 2.

13 Industry4Europe, 'A Long-Term Strategy for Europe's Industrial Future: From Words to Action' (November 2019) <www.industry4europe.eu/assets/Uploads/Publications/Industry4Europe_Joint-Paper_November-2019.pdf> accessed 31 July 2020, 25.

14 The full text of the letter is accessible at Elisa Braun, Thibault Larger and Simon Van Dorpe, 'EU Big Four Press Vestager to Clear Path for Champions' (Politico, 6 February 2020) <www.politico.eu/article/eu-big-four-france-germany-italy-poland-press-executive-vice-president-margrethe-vestager-to-clear-path-for-champions/> accessed 31 July 2020.

It should be noted that the aforementioned proposals have been opposed by several stakeholder groups, including the academic community and national competition authorities. In an open letter authored by competition policy scholars Massimo Motta (Barcelona Graduate School of Economics) and Martin Peitz (University of Mannheim), the authors argued that 'competition policy should be independent from political interference based on perceived European industrial goals, and respond to efficiency considerations and the protection of the competitive process'.[15] Along the same lines were the concerns voiced by the Austrian competition authority: 'creation of supposed national or European champions holds the danger of arbitrary regulatory decision-making and, as a result of this, would ultimately harm European and Austrian companies more than it would benefit them'.[16]

In its policy document concerning external relations with China, the Commission recognized that 'EU merger control does not allow the Commission to intervene against the acquisition of a European company solely on the grounds that the buyer benefitted from foreign subsidies'.[17] As a result, the Commission pledged to 'identify before the end of the year [2019] how to fill gaps in EU law in order to address fully the distortive effects of foreign state ownership and state-aid financing in the Single Market'.[18] The Dutch government has identified that gap in the absence of the state aid and antitrust enforcement at the global level and proposed to supplement the existing regulatory framework of the EU competition law with a level-playing-field mechanism.[19] According to the Dutch proposal, if a company, irrespective of its nationality, distorts or threatens to distort competition in the internal market due to government support or an unregulated dominant position in a third-country market, then the Commission may impose certain limitations on the economic activities of such company within the internal market.[20] Such limitations could include prohibitions on (1) supply

15 'Open Letter: More, Not Less, Competition Is Needed in Europe' (10 February 2019) <www.competitionpolicyinternational.com/more-not-less-competition-is-needed-in-europe/> accessed 31 July 2020.

16 Federal Competition Authority (Austria), 'Position Paper on National and European Champions in Merger Control' (November 2019), <www.bwb.gv.at/fileadmin/user_upload/PDFs/Positionspapier_European_Champions_EN.pdf> accessed 31 July 2020, 25.

17 EU Commission, Joint Communication to the European Parliament, the European Council, and the Council 'EU-China: A Strategic Outlook' JOIN (2019) 5 final, 12 March 2019, 8.

18 General Secretariat of the Council, European Council meeting (21 and 22 March 2019) – Conclusions, EUCO 1/19, <www.consilium.europa.eu/media/38789/22-euco-final-conclusions-en.pdf> accessed 31 July 2020, 2.

19 See Dutch Permanent Representation to the EU, 'Non-Paper Strengthening the Level Playing Field on the Internal Market' (9 December 2019) <www.permanentrepresentations.nl/documents/publications/2019/12/09/non-paper-on-level-playing-field> accessed 31 July 2020.

20 Ibid., 2.

constraints that are not in line with market conditions; (2) price and product differentiation between different market operators on comparable transactions; (3) tied selling, whereby additional conditions are imposed with no (apparent) relationship to the transaction; (4) wholesale/retail pricing that is not a reflection of market prices and/or production costs; (5) investments in assets with no apparent business case, i.e. that are insufficiently profitable.[21]

On 10 March 2020, the Commission released a string of policy documents comprising a New Industrial Strategy for Europe.[22] It stated that 'an independent EU competition policy has served Europe well by helping to level the playing field, driving innovation and giving consumers more choice'.[23] In its plan to review the existing EU competition rules, the EU Commission mentioned the revision of the rules governing horizontal and vertical agreements. The policy document does not propose to reform the existing EU merger control rules. Instead, the Commission decided to pursue a distinct legal instrument that would address the distortive effects of the foreign subsidies in the EU internal market. For that purpose, the Commission published the White Paper on foreign subsidies on 17 June 2020 and pledged to come up with a legislative proposal in 2021.[24] The Commission's approach demonstrates its unwillingness to bend the EU merger control regime in order to accommodate the industrial policy aspirations of certain Member States in order to stimulate the establishment of the 'European champions'.[25] The Commission has clearly opted in favor of trade defense mechanisms and the investment screening coordination, which will be further discussed in the present chapter.

4.2 National merger control regimes and 'public interest' considerations

There is no universal definition or list of public interest considerations. Public policy goals significantly differ from one jurisdiction to another, depending

---

21 Ibid.
22 EU Commission, press release IP/20/416 'Making Europe's Businesses Future-Ready: A New Industrial Strategy for a Globally Competitive, Green and Digital Europe' (10 March 2020) <https://ec.europa.eu/commission/presscorner/detail/en/ip_20_416> accessed 31 July 2020.
23 EU Commission, COM(2020) 102 final, A New Industrial Strategy for Europe (10 March 2020), 5.
24 Ibid., 6.
25 See Alexandr Svetlicinii, 'The Interactions of Competition Law and Investment Law: The Case of Chinese State-Owned Enterprises and EU Merger Control Regime', in Julien Chaisse, Leïla Choukroune and Sufian Jusoh (eds.) *Handbook of International Investment Law and Policy* (Springer, 2019), 21.

on the social, cultural and political context and may change over time to reflect social developments.[26]

The EU merger control regime administered under the EUMR provided a one-stop-shop for the economic concentrations that reach the 'Community dimension' calculated on the basis of the relevant annual turnover of the undertakings concerned.[27] Once the relevant turnover thresholds are met, the concentration has to be notified to the Commission for assessment.[28] In cases where a concentration threatens to affect significantly competition in a market within a particular Member State, which presents all the characteristics of a distinct market, the Commission may refer the concentration to the NCA of the Member State concerned.[29] Concentrations that do not reach the 'Community dimension' may still be notifiable under the national merger control rules of the Member States. As a result, a significant number of merger cases are handled by the NCAs under the national merger control rules. A review of the 28 national merger control regimes in the EU Member States allows to identify three broader groups of jurisdictions according to their assessment of the SOE-related mergers and acquisitions: (1) countries with no specific rules for SOE-related concentrations; (2) countries with specific rules or guidelines concerning the SOE-related concentrations; (3) countries with sector-specific merger control rules.[30]

The Member States that belong to the first group generally follow the Commission's approach under the EUMR by determining whether the SOEs owned by the same state belong to a single economic unit due to the coordination of their commercial activities from the same center of decision. For example, in France, the merger control guidelines refer to recital 22 of the EUMR establishing the principle of non-discrimination between private and state owned entities.[31] Likewise, in Slovakia, the guidelines on

26 Organisation for Economic Co-Operation and Development, 'Executive Summary of the Roundtable on Public Interest Considerations in Merger Control', DAF/COMP/WP3/M (2016)1/ANN5/FINAL (20 March 2017) <https://one.oecd.org/document/DAF/COMP/WP3/M(2016)1/ANN5/FINAL/en/pdf> accessed 31 July 2020, 2.
27 EUMR, Article 1(2).
28 Ibid., Article 4.
29 Ibid., Article 9.
30 See Alexandr Svetlicinii, 'The Acquisitions of the Chinese State-Owned Enterprises under the National Merger Control Regimes of the EU Member States: Searching for a Coherent Approach' (2018) 2 *Market and Competition Law Review* 99.
31 *Lignes directrices de l'Autorité de la concurrence relatives au contrôle des concentrations* (10 July 2013) <www.autoritedelaconcurrence.fr/sites/default/files/ld_concentrations_juill13.pdf> accessed 31 July 2020, para 108.

the calculation of the relevant turnover refer to the Commission's Jurisdictional Notice when discussing how to calculate the turnover of the SOEs.[32]

The second group includes Denmark, which adopted several SOE-related rules concerning the calculation of the relevant turnover. If an SOE is controlled by the central government, the turnover is replaced by the aggregate gross operational expenditure in the preceding accounting year of the ministerial province concerned and in the central government accounts.[33] For a municipal or regional authority, the turnover is replaced by the aggregate gross operational and investment expenditure in the preceding accounting year.[34] In the Czech Republic, the NCA has issued guidelines specifying that 'if the state company is not part of a broad industrial holding company and is not subject to any coordination with other state-controlled companies, it must be considered an independent entity for the purpose of turnover calculation'.[35] Similarly, the Estonian NCA will depart from the presumption that 'if the state or a local government controls an undertaking, such undertaking shall not be deemed to be related through control to other undertakings controlled by the state or local government' only in a situation where 'such undertakings are jointly managed by a holding company established for such purpose or their economic activities are directed jointly in another manner'.[36]

For example, in Hungary, the Competition Act specifies that 'in calculating the net turnover of undertakings in majority state or municipal ownership, those undertakings constituting economic units shall be taken into account which have autonomous decision-making powers in determining their market conduct'.[37] The following example demonstrates how this rule is applied in the practice of the Hungarian Competition Authority. In 2012, the Hungarian NCA cleared the transfer of shares from one SOE (Magyar Villamos Művek Zrt., or MVM) to another SOE (MFB Invest Befektetési

---

32 Anti-Monopoly Office, Guidelines on Calculation of Turnover (1 July 2014) <www.antimon.gov.sk/data/files/387_usmernenie-protimonopolneho-uradu-slovenskej-republiky-k-vypoctu-obratu.pdf> accessed 31 July 2020, para 28.

33 See Executive Order No. 808 of 14 August 2009 on the Calculation of Turnover in the Competition Act, <www.en.kfst.dk/media/1366/executive-order-on-the-calculation-of-turnover-in-the-competition-act.pdf> accessed 31 July 2020, para 9(1).

34 Ibid., para 9(2).

35 Office for the Protection of Competition, Notice on Calculation of Turnover for the Purpose of the Control of Concentrations between Undertakings <www.uohs.cz/en/competition/decisions-guidelines-and-other-documents.html> accessed 31 July 2020, para 42.

36 Minister of Economic Affairs and Communications, Guidelines for Calculation of Turnover of Parties to Concentration (17 July 2006) <www.riigiteataja.ee/en/eli/ee/MKM/reg/522042016004/> accessed 31 July 2020, para 19.

37 Act LVII of 1996 on the prohibition of unfair and restrictive market practices (as applicable from 1 January 2019), Article 27(3).

és Vagyonkezelő Zrt., or MFB Invest), which resulted in their joint control over Magyar Gáz Tranzit Zrt., which was previously under the single control of MVM.[38] Both SOEs were controlled by the Minister for Economic Development through Hungarian National Management Zrt. The Hungarian NCA conducted an assessment of the exercise of state control over the commercial decision making of the two SOEs. Because, in relation to MFB Invest, the rights of the Minister were restricted to the approval of business plans, the NCA concluded that the two SOEs did not belong to the same decision-making center and should be regarded as independent entities for the purpose of merger assessment.[39]

The lack of detailed guidelines on the assessment of SOE-related concentrations is accompanied by scarce attention attributed to the SOE status in the NCAs' merger decisions. For example, in 2013, China Merchants Holdings (International) Co Ltd., a subsidiary of China Merchants Group, notified its investment in Terminal Link SAS, a container terminals operator, to the Cypriot NCA. The NCA's decision refers to the acquiring undertaking as 'an important investor and operator of ports in China and one of the largest operators of public ports in China, holding shares in fifteen terminals companies'[40] but does not mention that China Merchants Group 'is a state-owned backbone enterprise headquartered in Hong Kong and is under the direct supervision of State-owned Assets Supervision and Administration Commission of the State Council (SASAC)'.[41] Similarly, in a 2012 merger case, the Czech NCA considered that the ultimate controlling entity of Weichai Power Co was Shandong Heavy Industry Group without addressing the role of the Shandong SASAC.[42] When assessing another concentration involving Weichai Holding Group Hong Kong Investment Co., the Italian NCA acknowledged the existence of control by the Shandong SASAC and considered the operations of other SOEs under the

---

38 Hungarian Competition Authority, Case Vj-23/2012, decision of 21 March 2012.

39 See Zsuzsanna Németh, 'The Hungarian Competition Authority Clears the Acquisition of the Prospective Owner and Operator of the Gas Interconnector between Slovakia and Hungary by Two State Owned Companies (*Magyar Villamos Művek / MFB Invest Befektetési és Vagyonkezelő / Magyar Gáz Tranzit*)' (2012) e-*Competitions* March 2012, Art. N° 49212 <www.concurrences.com/en/bulletin/news-issues/march-2012/the-hungarian-competition-authority-clears-the-acquisition-of-the-prospective-en> accessed 31 July 2020.

40 Commission for the Protection of Competition (Cyprus), Decision No. 16/2013 of 4 March 2013. In its Decision No. 66/2013 of 21 October 2013, the Cypriot NCA has acknowledged that China Shipping Terminal Development (Hong Kong) Co Ltd. was a Hong Kong subsidiary of China Shipping Group, SOE under the control of the Central SASAC.

41 China Merchants Group, Introduction, <http://www.cmhk.com/main/a/2016/a26/a30448_30530.shtml> accessed 31 July 2020.

42 Office for Protection of Competition (Czech Republic), Decision No. ÚOHS-S647/2012/KS-22387/2012/840/LBř of 27 November 2012.

control of the same regional SASAC.[43] The selective review of the NCAs' decisions in merger cases involving Chinese SOEs indicates 'that the issues of State ownership and control receive even less attention than in the cases examined by the EU Commission'.[44] As a result, in the absence of more detailed guidance from the Commission, there is a substantial degree of divergence in the NCAs' practice of assessing SOE-related concentrations under the national merger control regimes.

Another important connection between the EUMR and the national regulatory regimes concerns the public interest exception embedded in Article 21(4) EUMR, which is also called the 'English clause': 'Member States may take appropriate measures to protect legitimate interests other than those taken into consideration by this Regulation and compatible with the general principles and other provisions of Community law'.[45] The legitimate interests include among others public security, plurality of the media, and prudential rules. The list of legitimate interests is not exclusive, but any other public interest measures have to be communicated to the Commission and receive the latter's confirmation that such measures comply with the general principles and other provisions of EU law. Such 'legitimate interests' will permit a Member State to block a concentration that would be otherwise cleared by the Commission or to impose certain remedies that would protect the legitimate interest of such Member State.

The EU Member States have invoked public security interest in merger cases concerning production and trade in arms, munitions, and war material, as well as those related to the security of supply of basic inputs such as water and electricity[46] (Annex III). The United Kingdom has invoked media plurality on several occasions to ensure the accurate presentation of the news and the free expression of opinion.[47] At the same time, the Commission has closely scrutinized 'other interests' notified by the Member States so as to prevent the disguised use of economic protectionism.[48]

---

43 Competition and Market Authority (Italy), Decision No. 23379 of 6 March 2012 in case C11502.
44 Svetlicinii, 'The Acquisitions of the Chinese State-Owned Enterprises under the National Merger Control Regimes of the EU Member States: Searching for a Coherent Approach', 116.
45 EUMR, Article 21(4).
46 Organisation for Economic Co-Operation and Development, 'Public Interest Considerations in Merger Control: Note by the European Union', DAF/COMP/WP3/WD(2016)11 (3 June 2016) <www.oecd.org/officialdocuments/publicdisplaydocumentpdf/?cote=DAF/COMP/WP3/WD(2016)11&docLanguage=En>, accessed 31 July 2020, 4.
47 See also Organisation for Economic Co-Operation and Development, 'Public Interest Considerations in Merger Control: Note by the United Kingdom', DAF/COMP/WP3/WD(2016)9 (27 May 2016) <www.oecd.org/officialdocuments/publicdisplaydocumentpdf/?cote=DAF/COMP/WP3/WD(2016)9&docLanguage=En> accessed 31 July 2020.
48 For Commission's practice under Article 21(4) EUMR see Hungarian Academy of Sciences, Centre for Social Sciences, Lendület-HPOPs Research Group, 'EU Merger Control and the

In 2000, the Portuguese government has used its golden shares in Cimpor Cimentos de Portugal to block the takeover on the ground of

> the need to protect the development of the shareholding structures in companies undergoing privatisation with a view to reinforcing the corporate capacity and the efficiency of the national production apparatus in a way that is consistent with the national economic policy guidelines.[49]

The Commission has not recognized this explanation as a legitimate public interest under Article 21(4) EUMR. Similarly, in the *BSCH/A. Champalimaud* case, the Commission did not permit the Portuguese government to block an acquisition of a Portuguese insurance company by a Spanish bank on the basis of 'national interest in strategic sectors'.[50] In the *Unicredito Italiano S.p.A./Bayerische Hypo-und Vereinsbank AG* case, the Commission did not allow the Polish government to use privatization rules in order to prevent acquisition of the Polish subsidiary Bank BPH SA.[51] The Italian government's attempts to use 'national economic interests' for blocking several takeovers in the banking industry were likewise rejected by the Commission.[52] The Commission's approach toward public interest exception in EU merger control resolutely opposed the use of disguised economic protectionism that would hinder the freedom of establishment in the EU.[53]

Public Interest' (2016) <https://hpops.tk.mta.hu/uploads/files/Merger.pdf> accessed 31 July 2020.

49 EU Commission, press release IP/00/1338 'Commission Rules against Portuguese Measures in a Takeover Bid for Cement Company Cimpor' (22 November 2000) <https://ec.europa.eu/commission/presscorner/detail/en/IP_00_1338> accessed 31 July 2020. See also Téa Makela, 'The EU Court of Justice Rules for the First Time on Article 21(3) of the Merger Regulation (*Portuguese Republic / Commission*)' (2004) *e-Competitions Judicial Review* Art. N° 37325 <www.concurrences.com/en/bulletin/special-issues/judicial-review/mergers/the-european-court-of-justice-rules-for-the-first-time-on-article-21-3-of-the> accessed 31 July 2020.

50 *Antonio De Sommer Champalimaud/Banco Santander Central Hispanoamericano* (Case No. IV/M.1616) [1999] OJ C306/37, decision of 20 July 1999.

51 *Unicredito/HVB* (Case No. COMP/M.3894) [2005] OJ C278/17, decision of 18 October 2005.

52 See *BBVA/BNL* (Case No. COMP/M.3768) [2005] OJ C135/2, decision of 27 April 2005, *ABN AMRO/Banca Antonveneta* (Case No. COMP/M.3780) [2005], decision of 27 April 2005. See also Elisa Zaera Cuadrado, 'The EU Commission Decides Not to Formally Intervene Following a Claim by Banks Bidding to Merge that the Italian Banking Regulator Created Obstacles to Their Respective Bids (*BBVA / ABN*)' (2005) *e-Competitions* April 2005, Art. N° 36756 <www.concurrences.com/en/bulletin/news-issues/april-2005/The-European-Commission-decides-36756> accessed 31 July 2020.

53 See also Anu Bradford, Robert J. Jackson Jr. and Jonathon Zytnick, 'Is E.U. Merger Control Used for Protectionism? An Empirical Analysis' (2018) 15 *Journal of Empirical Legal Studies* 165.

One should also note the functioning of the national merger control regimes, which include public interest considerations that may differ from those listed in Article 21(4) EUMR. A recent study comparing the merger control regimes of Austria, France, Germany, and the UK concluded that the broad definition of non-market public interests 'offers scope for injecting vested interests of politicians, companies and other powerful lobbies into the decision process in the guise of ostensible "public" interest'.[54] An earlier, and a more extensive, study found that national merger control regimes of at least 12 Member States 'differ considerably in terms of how, when and by whom public interest considerations are taken into account as what grounds can be relied upon'.[55] On that background it was argued that

> the Merger Regulation's nod toward public interests appears somewhat limited and unduly defensive in nature, thereby acting as a frustrating impediment to Member States seeking to harness competition to promote European industry at home and abroad to the benefit of the Single Market.[56]

The existence of the national merger control regimes with the distinct public interest consideration mechanisms leaves substantial room for divergent merger control enforcement in relation to the Chinese SOE acquisitions by the individual Member States. This divergence could be partially addressed by a more detailed guidance[57] on SOE-related mergers that should be issued by the European Competition Network to assist the NCAs in determining the scope of a 'single economic unit' in SOE-related concentrations and in assessing the (anti)competitive effects of such mergers. However, such guidance would not affect the use of public interest interventions in the merger assessment, which could attain special significance in cases involving Chinese SOEs. These interventions could be 'employed as

---

54 Oliver Budzinski and Annika Stöhr, 'Public Interest Considerations in European Merger Control Regimes' (2019) 25 *Ilmenau Economics Discussion Papers* No.13 <www.econ stor.eu/bitstream/10419/203144/1/1671887840.pdf> accessed 31 July 2020, 26.

55 EU Merger Working Group, 'Public Interest Regimes in the European Union – Differences and Similarities in Approach' (10 March 2016) <https://ec.europa.eu/competition/ecn/ mwg_public_interest_regimes_en.pdf> accessed 31 July 2020, para 10.

56 Alex Nourry and Dani Rabinowitz, 'European Champions: What Now for EU Merger Control after Siemens/Alstom?' (2020) 41 *European Competition Law Review* 116, 120.

57 This could be done in the form of the best practices compilation, similar to EU Merger Working Group, 'Best Practices on Cooperation between EU National Competition Authorities in Merger Review' (8 November 2011), <https://ec.europa.eu/competition/ecn/ nca_best_practices_merger_review_en.pdf> accessed 31 July 2020.

the legal basis for the decisions of the relevant authorities and do not override identified competition concerns'.[58]

4.3 Foreign investment screening in the EU: building a coordination mechanism

If the looming presence of China helps shape the contours of the new EU policy on investment, in turn the EU might increasingly shape the contours of the global rules on investment.[59]

The Chinese SOEs' investments in Europe have been addressed by the Commission in its overall strategy toward China in the following way: '[i]t is important for the EU to work with China to promote open and fair competition in each other's markets and to discourage China from underwriting its companies' competitiveness through subsidisation or the protection of domestic markets'.[60] The European Parliament has also expressed its concerns about the Chinese SOEs' acquisitions: 'such investments are part of an overall strategy to have Chinese state-controlled or state-funded companies take control of banking and the energy sector, as well as other supply chains'.[61] As a result, the Commission's 2019 policy paper 'EU-China – A Strategic Outlook' has regarded China as 'an economic competitor in the pursuit of technological leadership, and a systemic rival promoting alternative models of governance',[62] which set the stage for a number of regulatory measures at the EU level. Among these measures was the adoption of the EU-wide mechanism for coordination of the FDI screening.

Already in 2017, the Commission tabled a proposal for a regulation establishing a framework to screen foreign direct investments from third countries on grounds of security and public order in the EU. In the accompanying communication document, the Commission noted the increased role of the SOEs in outward investment flows of non-EU countries and also witnessed the 'situations whereby certain companies are directly or

58 Mateusz Blachucki, 'Public Interest Considerations in Merger Control Assessment' (2014) 35 *European Competition Law Review* 380, 384.
59 Sophie Meunier, 'Divide and Conquer? China and the Cacophony of Foreign Investment Rules in the EU' (2014) 21 *Journal of European Public Policy* 996, 1013.
60 EU Commission, Joint Communication to the European Parliament, and the Council "Elements for a New EU Strategy on China" JOIN (2016) 30 final (22 June 2016), 6.
61 European Parliament resolution of 12 September 2018 on the state of EU-China Relations (2017/2274(INI)), para 8.
62 EU Commission, Joint Communication to the European Parliament, the European Council, and the Council 'EU-China – A Strategic Outlook' JOIN (2019) 5 final, 12 March 2019, 1.

indirectly influenced by the state through various means, or where the state facilitates foreign take-overs by national companies, notably through facilitating access to financing below market rates'.[63]

During the public consultation on the proposal for the EU FDI Screening Regulation, the Commission has received the requests to 'assess whether the current EU mergers and takeovers rules needs to be reviewed for a better efficiency of the objectives of the proposal' for FDI screening framework.[64] When explaining the relationship between the proposed FDI screening regime and the merger control regime under the EUMR, the Commission noted that 'assessment of the compatibility of a notified concentration carried out under the EU Merger Regulation focuses solely on competition and does not take into account security or public order concerns'.[65] This statement reflects the Commission's approach to the aforementioned proposals to reform to the EU merger control rules in order to make them more efficient in countering anti-competitive effects that could be raised by the foreign SOEs' acquisitions.

In its 2019 study on the foreign investment flows into the EU, the Commission considered all Chinese acquisitions to be linked to the Chinese government, because (1) investments are usually authorized by the government and targeted to specific sectors (e.g. those covering the China 2025 strategy) and (2) investments generally involve loans given by Chinese banks (most of them directly controlled by the government).[66] The Commission noted that the state influence over SOEs may lead them 'to acquire an EU company for strategic, rather than purely commercial, reasons, while State support may result, for instance, in their ability to pay more than other potential domestic or third-country acquirers might'.[67]

---

63 EU Commission, Welcoming Foreign Direct Investment while Protecting Essential Interests, COM(2017) 494 final (13 September 2017), 5.

64 Federation of European Private Port Operators and Terminals, 'FEPORT Reply to Consultation Concerning the Proposal for a Regulation of the European Parliament and of the Council Establishing a Framework for Screening of Foreign Direct Investments into the European Union' (COM (2017)487) (12 December 2017) <https://ec.europa.eu/info/law/better-regulation/have-your-say/initiatives/1084-REGULATION-OF-THE-EUROPEAN-PARLIAMENT-AND-OF-THE-COUNCIL-establishing-a-framework-to-review-FDIs-into-the-EU/F8152> accessed 31 July 2020, 3.

65 Ibid., 8.

66 EU Commission, Commission Staff Working Document on Foreign Direct Investment in the EU Following Up on the Commission's Communication 'Welcoming Foreign Direct Investment while Protecting Essential Interests' of 13 September 2017, SWD(2019) 108 final (13 March 2019), 56.

67 Ibid., 61.

The EU FDI Screening Regulation[68] was adopted by the EU Council on 5 March 2019. Despite the fact that the Commission had no prior experience with conducting the security screening of the FDI, the regulation was passed without a prior comprehensive impact assessment, which was justified by the sense of urgency and the growing concerns of the Member States.[69] The public consultation on the legislative proposal for the EU FDI Screening Regulation lasted four months (September to December 2017) but generated only three feedback submissions from the industry associations.[70] This apparent lack of attention to this important legislative development stands in stark contrast with the preceding calls for counteracting foreign SOE acquisitions voiced by the Member States' governments and other stakeholders. Although entering into force in April 2019,[71] the EU FDI Screening Regulation has become fully operational on 11 October 2020. The Commission has urged the Member States to 'detect and raise awareness of security risks posed by foreign investment in critical assets, technologies and infrastructure, Member States should ensure the swift, full and effective implementation of the Regulation on screening of foreign direct investment'.[72]

Although the FDI screening on the basis of national security and public order remains in the exclusive competence of the Member States, the EU FDI Screening Regulation does not introduce an obligation for the Member States to adopt or adjust FDI screening rules.[73] The FDI is defined as 'lasting and direct links between the foreign investor and the entrepreneur to whom or the undertaking to which the capital is made available in order

---

68 Regulation 2019/452 of 19 March 2019 establishing a framework for the screening of foreign direct investments into the Union, OJ L179/1, 21 March 2019.
69 See Leonie Reins, 'The European Union's Framework for FDI Screening: Towards an Ever More Growing Competence over Energy Policy?' (2019) 128 *Energy Policy* 665, 668. For arguments questioning the legal basis of the EU FDI Screening Regulation see Bin Ye, 'Comments on EU's Proposed Regulation on Establishing a European Framework for Screening FDI: Right Legal Basis?' (2018) 4 *EU-China Observer* 9.
70 These submissions are available at <https://ec.europa.eu/info/law/better-regulation/have-your-say/initiatives/1084-REGULATION-OF-THE-EUROPEAN-PARLIAMENT-AND-OF-THE-COUNCIL-establishing-a-framework-to-review-FDIs-into-the-EU> accessed 31 July 2020.
71 EU Commission, press release IP/19/2088 'EU Foreign Investment Screening Regulation Enters Into Force' (10 April 2019) <https://ec.europa.eu/commission/presscorner/detail/en/IP_19_2088> accessed 31 July 2020.
72 EU Commission, Joint Communication to the European Parliament, the European Council, and the Council 'EU-China: A Strategic Outlook' JOIN (2019) 5 final (12 March 2019), 10.
73 Regulation 2019/452, Article 1(3).

to carry on an economic activity in a Member State',[74] which covers both participation in and control of a company.

The EU FDI Screening Regulation introduced the following criteria, which may be taken into account by the Member States in the process of FDI screening: (1) critical infrastructure;[75] (2) critical technologies;[76] (3) critical inputs;[77] (4) access to sensitive information including personal data; (5) freedom and pluralism of the media. The following characteristics of the foreign investor may be taken into account: (1) whether the foreign investor is directly or indirectly controlled by the government, including state bodies or armed forces, of a third country, including through ownership structure or significant funding; (2) whether the foreign investor has already been involved in activities affecting security or public order in a Member State; (3) whether there is a serious risk that the foreign investor engages in illegal or criminal activities.[78] Although item (1) clearly points to the SOEs and other state-controlled entities, the EU FDI Screening Regulation leaves it to the Member States to develop further criteria on how the state control of foreign investor should be assessed. It generally allows

> Member States and the Commission to take into account the context and circumstances of the foreign direct investment, in particular whether a foreign investor is controlled directly or indirectly, for example through significant funding, including subsidies, by the government of a third country or is pursuing State-led outward projects or programmes.[79]

During the public consultation process, this general distinction between state owned and private companies was criticized for the lack of any 'meaningful and applicable criteria on how national legislation can make such a distinction'.[80]

---

74 Ibid., Article 2(1).
75 Ibid., Article 4(1)(a). Critical infrastructure includes energy, transport, water, health, communications, media, data processing or storage, aerospace, defense, electoral or financial infrastructure, and sensitive facilities, as well as land and real estate crucial for the use of such infrastructure.
76 Ibid., Article 4(1)(b). Critical technologies include artificial intelligence, robotics, semiconductors, cybersecurity, aerospace, defense, energy storage, quantum and nuclear technologies as well as nanotechnologies and biotechnologies.
77 Ibid., Article 4(1)(c). Critical inputs include energy or raw materials, as well as food security.
78 Ibid., Article 4(2).
79 Ibid., recital 13.
80 Federation of German Industries (BDI), 'Screening Foreign Direct Investment? Position on the Proposed EU Regulation Establishing a Framework for Screening of Foreign Direct Investments into the European Union' (12 December 2017) <https://ec.europa.eu/info/law/better-regulation/have-your-say/initiatives/1084-REGULATION-OF-THE-EUROPEAN-PARLIAMENT-AND-OF-THE-COUNCIL-establishing-a-framework-to-review-FDIs-into-

The EU FDI Screening Regulation established an obligation of the Member State undertaking FDI screening to inform the Commission and other Member States.[81] Any Member State that considers itself to be affected by the foreign investor undergoing screening may provide comments to the Member State that is undertaking the screening.[82] Similarly, the Commission can provide opinions in cases where it considers that the foreign investment under screening 'is likely to affect security or public order in more than one Member State'[83] or when the foreign investment concerns 'projects or programmes of Union interest'.[84] The Member State undertaking the screening should 'give due consideration' to such comments and/or opinions when taking the final decision.[85] The EU FDI Screening Regulation also authorizes the Commission and the Member States concerned to provide their opinions and comments on the planned or completed foreign investments that did not undergo the FDI screening.[86] Because the information about such investments may come from the annual reports submitted by the Member States, the comments and opinions can be provided within the period of 15 months following the completion of such investments.[87]

The EU FDI Screening Regulation has thus introduced an additional level of regulatory scrutiny for the transactions that may also fall under the EUMR. The definition of 'foreign investment' under Regulation 2019/452 is significantly wider because it is not limited to acquisitions of control or by any turnover thresholds, which may be set at the level of individual Member States. As a result, the concentrations reaching the 'Community dimension' under the EUMR may be also reviewed under the Regulation 2019/452 by one or more Member States and the Commission. As far as the criteria

---

the-EU/F8162> accessed 31 July 2020, 8. Other stakeholders, such as the Austrian Federal Economic Chamber (WKÖ), have welcomed the inclusion of the state support as a legitimate FDI screening criterion. The WKÖ's position is available at <https://ec.europa.eu/info/law/better-regulation/have-your-say/initiatives/1084-REGULATION-OF-THE-EUROPEAN-PARLIAMENT-AND-OF-THE-COUNCIL-establishing-a-framework-to-review-FDIs-into-the-EU/F8154> accessed 31 July 2020.

81 Regulation 2019/452, Article 6(1).
82 Ibid., Article 6(2).
83 Ibid., Article 6(3).
84 Ibid., Article 8. Projects or programs of Union interest include: (1) European GNSS programs (Galileo and EGNOS): (2) Copernicus; (3) Horizon 2020; (4) Trans-European Networks for Transport (TEN-T); (5) Trans-European Networks for Energy (TEN-E); (6) Trans-European Networks for Telecommunications; (7) European Defence Industrial Development Programme; (8) Permanent Structured Cooperation (PESCO); (9) Preparatory Action on Preparing the new EU GOVSATCOM programme; (10) Preparatory Action on Defence Research; (11) European Joint Undertaking for ITER.
85 Ibid., Article 6(9).
86 Ibid., Article 7.
87 Ibid., Article 7(8).

for review are concerned, the EUMR and the EU FDI Screening Regulation may overlap with reference to the public interest exceptions under Article 21(4) EUMR and the assessment criteria under the Regulation 2019/452 as specified in the national FDI screening legislation of the Member States (Annex IV). In this regard, the EU FDI Screening Regulation requires that

> the grounds for screening set out in Article 1 of this Regulation and the notion of legitimate interests within the meaning of the third paragraph of Article 21(4) of [EUMR] should be interpreted in a coherent manner, without prejudice to the assessment of the compatibility of the national measures aimed at protecting those interests with the general principles and other provisions of Union law.[88]

4.4 COVID-19 pandemic and further restrictions for FDI in the EU

> *As in any crisis, when our industrial and corporate assets can be under stress, we need to protect our security and economic sovereignty. We have the tools to deal with this situation under European and national law and I want to urge Member States to make full use of them. The EU is and will remain an open market for foreign direct investment. But this openness is not unconditional.[89]*

The COVID-19 pandemic, which was declared by the Director-General of the World Health Organization on 11 March 2020,[90] has prompted a string of regulatory measures introducing new restrictions on trade and investment. For instance, in order to address shortages with medical supplies and personal protective equipment, on 11 March 2020, the Commission made the exportation of certain products subject to market authorizations to be issued by the Member States concerned.[91] At their emergency meeting

---

88 Ibid., recital 36.
89 EU Commission, 'Coronavirus: Commission Issues Guidelines to Protect Critical European Assets and Technology in Current Crisis' (25 March 2020) <https://trade.ec.europa.eu/doclib/press/index.cfm?id=2124> accessed 31 July 2020.
90 World Health Organization, 'WHO Director-General's Opening Remarks at the Media Briefing on COVID-19' (11 March 2020) <www.consilium.europa.eu/media/43072/final-g20-leaders-statement-26032020.pdf> accessed 31 July 2020.
91 See Commission Implementing Regulation (EU) 2020/402 of 14 March 2020 making the exportation of certain products subject to production of an export authorization, OJ LI 77/1; guidance note to Member States of 20 March 2020 related to Commission Implementing Regulation (EU) 2020/402 making the exportation of certain products subject to

convened by Saudi Arabia on 26 March 2020, the leaders of the G20 group declared that their goal is 'to realize a free, fair, non-discriminatory, transparent, predictable and stable trade and investment environment, and to keep our markets open'.[92] Nevertheless, numerous trade restrictions remained in force and on 30 March 2020, the World Trade Organization reported various forms of trade and trade-related measures taken in the context of the COVID-19 crisis from 16 countries around the globe.[93]

In the EU, the emergency restrictions on foreign investments first appeared at the level of individual Member States as a part of the economic support measures directed toward their domestic companies and consumers (Annex IV). For example, on 17 March 2020, Spain adopted Royal Decree-Law 8/2020, which introduced additional restrictions on the FDI coming outside the EU/EEA.[94] This emergency measure was adopted in response to the economic disruptions caused by anti-epidemic measures. It introduced an approval regime for any FDI acquisitions exceeding 10% of the share capital of a Spanish company active in the areas that affect public order, public safety, and public health. These sectors included, in particular, (1) critical infrastructures, whether physical or virtual (including infrastructures of energy, transport, water, health care, communications, data treatment or storage, aerospace, defense, electoral or financial, and other sensitive facilities), as well as land and properties that are necessary for the use of the said infrastructures; (2) critical technologies and dual-use products (artificial intelligence, robotics, semiconductors, cybersecurity, aerospace, defense, energy storage, quantum and nuclear technology, as well as nanotechnologies and biotechnologies); (3) supply of fundamental inputs, in particular energy, hydrocarbons, and food; (4) sectors with access to sensitive information such as personal data; and (5) media.[95]

---

the production of an export authorization, as last amended by Commission Implementing Regulation (EU) 2020/426, OJ C91/10.

92 Extraordinary G20 Leaders' Summit, 'Statement on COVID-19' (26 March 2020) <www. ilo.org/global/about-the-ilo/how-the-ilo-works/multilateral-system/g20/WCMS_740022/ lang-en/index.htm> accessed on 31 July 2020.

93 World Trade Organization, 'COVID-19: Trade and Trade-Related Measures' (as of 14 April 2020) <www.wto.org/english/tratop_e/covid19_e/covid_measures_e.pdf> accessed 31 July 2020.

94 Royal Decree-Law 8/2020 of 17 March 2020, <www.boe.es/boe/dias/2020/03/18/pdfs/ BOE-A-2020-3824.pdf> accessed 31 July 2020. Royal Decree-Law 11/2020 of 31 March 2020 has further specified that the term 'foreign investors' covers also the companies registered in the EU/EEA, but controlled by an entity registered outside the EU/EEA or an EU/ EEA company where the foreign investor's participation exceeds 25% of the share capital.

95 Royal Decree-Law 8/2020.

The *ex ante* approval will be also necessary for the following types of FDI: (1) when the foreign investor is controlled directly or indirectly by the government of a third country, including public bodies or armed forces; (2) when the foreign investor has invested or participated in sectors affecting the security, public order, or public health in another Member State; (3) if an administrative or judicial proceeding has been launched against the foreign investor in another Member State or in the state of origin or in a third country for carrying out criminal or other illegal activities.[96] The Decree-Law 8/2020 also authorized the government to suspend the investment liberalization regime in other sectors when the FDI may affect public order, public safety, or public health. It was argued that the preceding restrictions could also be applied in cases of indirect FDI, when an acquisition of control triggered by an indirect acquisition outside of Spain will be subjected to authorization by Spanish authorities.[97]

The regulatory steps to restrict FDI from the third countries undertaken by Spanish authorities have been also considered in the Commission's policy documents. In its initial communication on the economic response to the COVID-19 pandemic, the Commission has called the Member States 'to be vigilant and use all tools available at Union and national level to avoid that the current crisis leads to a loss of critical assets and technology'.[98] The expression 'all tools available' should be read in the Commission's Guidance to the Member States concerning foreign direct investment and free movement of capital from third countries, and the protection of Europe's strategic assets, ahead of the application of FDI Screening Regulation.[99]

The Commission explained that the economic shock caused by the pandemic disruptions presented an increased potential risk for strategic industries, including the health care sector. In such circumstances, according to the Commission, 'there could be an increased risk of attempts to acquire healthcare capacities (for example for the productions of medical or protective equipment) or related industries such as research establishments (for instance developing vaccines) via foreign direct investment'.[100] The

---

96 Ibid.

97 See Callol, Coca & Associados, Regulatory Advisory (Foreign Investment Screening) (18 March 2020) <http://callolcoca.com/regulatory-alert-march-2020-2/> accessed 31 July 2020.

98 EU Commission, 'Coordinated Economic Response to the COVID-19 Outbreak', COM (2020) 112 final (3 March 2020), 2.

99 EU Commission, guidance to the Member States concerning foreign direct investment and free movement of capital from third countries, and the protection of Europe's strategic assets, ahead of the application of Regulation (EU) 2019/452, C(2020) 1981 final (25 March 2020).

100 Ibid., 1.

volatility or undervaluation of European stock markets could also expose other critical sectors and infrastructure to possible foreign acquisitions. As explained by the EU trade commissioner Phil Hogan,

> [w]e need to know who invests and for what purpose. The EU and its Member States have the right legal tools for that. Today's guidelines call upon Member States to use these tools to the fullest extent and will bring additional clarity on how to use our investment screening frame-work to prevent a sell-off of strategic EU assets in the current crisis.[101]

To this he added: '[r]emember, the acquisition of a company in your country may have a security effect in other member states or it may negatively affect a project of union interest'.[102]

To address the aforementioned risks, the Commission urged the Member States to make full use of their national FDI screening mechanisms. For those Member States that do not yet have such mechanisms in place, the Commission recommended

> to set up a full-fledged screening mechanism and in the meantime to use all other available options to address cases where the acquisition or control of a particular business, infrastructure or technology would create a risk to security or public order in the EU, including a risk to critical health infrastructures and supply of critical inputs.[103]

Although, the EU FDI Screening Regulation does not require Member States to have an FDI screening regime in place, it nevertheless allows the Commission and the Member States concerned to provide comments and opinions during the period of 15 months after an investment has been completed without undergoing a screening.[104] This effectively means that if there is an investment completed without screening in March 2020, it could be subject to *ex post* comments and opinions until June 2021.[105]

The Commission's guidance has laid out a number of directions that should be followed by the Member States when designing or enforcing their

---

101 EU Commission, press release IP/20/528 'Coronavirus: Commission Issues Guidelines to Protect Critical European Assets and Technology in Current Crisis (25 March 2020) <https://ec.europa.eu/commission/presscorner/detail/en/ip_20_528> accessed 31 July 2020.

102 Jim Brunsden, 'EU Trade Chief Urges Tougher Defences Against Foreign Takeovers' (Financial Times, 17 April 2020), <www.ft.com/content/bf83fa94-1bcf-4532-a75a-50f41351c0d4> accessed 31 July 2020.

103 Guidance, 2.

104 Regulation 2019/452, Article 7(8).

105 Guidance, Annex, 2.

screening regimes under the EU FDI Regulation. First, the Commission suggested that the need to screen a transaction should not be based on its value: '[s]mall start-ups, for instance, may have a relatively limited value but may be of strategic importance on issues like research or technology'.[106] Second, the guidance urges the Member States to prevent the sell-off of industrial enterprises, including SMEs.

Third, the Commission suggested that besides possible prohibition of the foreign acquisitions, the Member States should consider other available remedies that should address national security and public interest considerations. For example, conditions guaranteeing the supply of medical products/devices can be imposed. In the health care sector, the Member States can also intervene 'by imposing compulsory licences on patented medicines in case of a national emergency such as a pandemic'.[107] Although several non-EU countries have already prepared legislative amendments for granting compulsory licenses on public health grounds,[108] the EU Member States have also started to contemplate the possibility of adopting a similar approach.[109]

Fourth, the Commission advised the Member States to make use of the 'golden shares' that may enable the state to block or set certain limits on the foreign investments in the companies where such 'golden shares' exist.[110] In that regard, the competition commissioner Vestager remarked: '[w]e don't have any issues of states acting as market participants if need be – if they provide shares in a company, if they want to prevent a takeover of this kind'.[111]

Fifth, the Commission pointed out that the FDI screening should not only cover acquisitions conferring control but also address minority shareholdings 'where they represent an acquisition of at least qualified shareholding that confers certain rights to the shareholder or connected shareholders under the national company law (e.g. 5%), they might be of relevance in

---

106 Ibid., Annex, 1.
107 Ibid., Annex, 2.
108 See Hilary Wong, 'The Case for Compulsory Licensing During COVID-19' *Journal of Global Health* <www.jogh.org/documents/issue202001/jogh-10-010358.htm> accessed 31 July 2020.
109 See Francois Pochart, Mathilde Rauline and Oceane de la Verteville, 'Compulsory Licenses Granted by Public Authorities: An Application in the Covid-19 Crisis in France? Part 1' (Kluwer Patent Blog, 23 April 2020) <http://patentblog.kluweriplaw.com/2020/04/23/compulsory-licenses-granted-by-public-authorities-an-application-in-the-covid-19-crisis-in-france-part-1/?doing_wp_cron=1594368198.0947930812835693 359375> accessed 31 July 2020.
110 Guidance, Annex, 3.
111 Javier Espinoza, 'Vestager Urges Stakebuilding to Block Chinese Takeovers' (Financial Times, 12 April 2020) <www.ft.com/content/e14f24c7-e47a-4c22-8cf3-f629da62b0a7> accessed 31 July 2020.

terms of security or public order'.[112] Italy, a country most severely affected by the pandemic, has followed the Commission's guidance and lowered the thresholds for screening of non-EU acquisitions in the strategic sectors to 10%.[113] Slovenia also adopted a 10% threshold for screening FDI in the strategic sectors.[114] Sixth, with reference to the CJEU jurisprudence, the Commission has noted that public interest justifications for restricting the movement of capital from the third countries should be interpreted more broadly than similar restrictions applied to the investments coming from other Member States.[115]

In the light of the COVID-19 pandemic, it should be expected that the Member States will accelerate both the implementation and the application of the FDI Screening Regulation: 'new EU Guidance Paper is likely to increase foreign investment screening activities at Member State level in the coming months and will also accelerate the introduction of new national legislation throughout the European Union'[116] (Annex IV). For example, on 8 April 2020, the German government passed a draft bill that puts in place the information sharing mechanism implementing the provisions of the EU FDI Screening Regulation.[117] On this occasion, the German legislator also reduced the standard for intervention under the FDI screening rules and extended the scope of the stand-still obligation for the transaction undergoing the scrutiny. In Italy, the government was reportedly contemplating the possibility of qualifying all Italian companies listed on the Milan Stock Exchange as strategic for the national economy, which would allow the prime minister to veto or impose conditions on the foreign investments targeting Italian listed companies.[118]

---

112 Guidance, Annex, 3.
113 Decree-Law No. 23 of 8 April 2020. See also Claudio Di Falco, 'Italy: COVID-19 Crisis Inspires Global Tightening of Foreign Investment Screening (Norton Rose Fulbright, 12 May 2020), <www.nortonrosefulbright.com/en/knowledge/publications/503220b7/italy> accessed 31 July 2020.
114 Law of 29 May 2020 on mitigation measures and elimination of consequences of COVID-19 epidemic, Official Gazette No. 80 of 30 May 2020, Article 70.
115 Guidance, Annex, 4.
116 Frank Röhling and others, 'COVID-19: Shut Down Also for Foreign Direct Investments into Europe? Commission Issues Guidance to Member States on How to Protect Strategic Assets' (Freshfields Bruckhaus Deringer, 27 March 2020) <https://transactions.freshfields.com/post/102g33i/covid-19-shut-down-also-for-foreign-direct-investments-into-europe-commission-i> accessed 31 July 2020.
117 See Frank Röhling, Uwe Salaschek and Jonas von Kalben, 'Germany to Introduce Stricter Foreign Investment Rules–Again (Freshfields Bruckhaus Deringer, 9 April 2020) <https://transactions.freshfields.com/post/102g4gi/germany-to-introduce-stricter-foreign-investment-rules-again> accessed 31 July 2020.
118 See Baker McKenzie, 'COVID-19: Impact on Governmental Foreign Investment Screening' (31 March 2020) <www.bakermckenzie.com/en/insight/publications/2020/03/covid19-impact-governmental-foreign> accessed 31 July 2020.

4.5 White Paper on foreign subsidies – an additional regulatory framework for foreign SOE investments in the EU

> *Along with other tools available at EU level such as foreign direct invest-ment screening and trade defence measures, the White Paper is a welcome addition to the toolbox for our open strategic autonomy.*[119]

On 17 June 2020, the Commission fulfilled its earlier commitment under the New Industrial Strategy for Europe[120] and published the White Paper on foreign subsidies, which unveiled a proposal for a regulatory instru-ment targeting foreign subsidies that distort competition in the internal market.[121] In the White Paper, the Commission refers to the regulatory gap in the EU competition law stating that 'neither EU antitrust rules nor EU merger control specifically take into account whether an economic operator may have benefited from foreign subsidies' and that the 'financial support granted by non-EU authorities to undertakings in the EU, either directly or through their parent companies outside the EU is not covered by EU State aid rules'.[122] As succinctly put by commissioner Vestager, 'our merger rules look at how a merger affects competition in Europe – but don't go into how that merger is paid for'.[123] Following the approach of the EU anti-subsidy regulation,[124] foreign subsidies are defined as

> financial contribution by a government or any public body of a non-EU State, which confers a benefit to a recipient and which is limited, in law or in fact, to an individual undertaking or industry or to a group of undertakings or industries.[125]

---

119 Phil Hogan, EU Commissioner for Trade, quoted in EU Commission, press release IP/20/1070 'Commission Adopts White Paper on Foreign Subsidies in the Single Mar-ket' (17 June 2020) <https://ec.europa.eu/commission/presscorner/detail/en/ip_20_1070> accessed 31 July 2020.

120 See EU Commission, 'A New Industrial Strategy for Europe' COM(2020) 102 final (10 March 2020), 6.

121 EU Commission, 'White Paper on Levelling the Playing Field as Regards Foreign Subsi-dies' COM(2020) 253 final (17 June 2020).

122 Ibid., para 3.1.

123 EU Commission, 'Statement by Executive Vice-President Margrethe Vestager on Adop-tion of White Paper on Foreign Subsidies in the Single Market' (17 June 2020) <https://ec.europa.eu/commission/presscorner/detail/en/statement_20_1121> accessed 31 July 2020.

124 Regulation 2016/1037 of the European Parliament and the Council of 8 June 2016 on protection against subsidized imports from countries not members of the European Union, OJ L176/55, 30 June 2016.

125 White Paper, Annex I.

The financial contribution may take various forms: (1) transfer of funds or liabilities; (2) foregone or not collected public revenue; (3) provision of goods or services or the purchase of goods and services.[126] The Commission proposed to use the benchmark of EUR 200,000, established in the EU state aid law,[127] to presume that foreign subsidies below that amount over a period of three years do not create distortions in the internal market.[128]

In order to fill the identified regulatory gap in the EU merger control, the Commission proposed a mechanism for screening of foreign subsidies facilitating the acquisition of EU targets.[129] The proposed mechanism includes the *ex ante* review of the planned acquisitions involving possible foreign subsidies by a competent supervisory authority. If, following an in-depth investigation, the supervisory authority determines that an acquisition was facilitated by foreign subsidies and distorts the internal market, it would accept commitments that remedy the distortion or prohibit the notified acquisition.[130] The Commission assumes that 'the parties would be aware if they have received any form of financial contribution from a third-country authority in the last three years'.[131] It should be noted that the coverage of the term 'acquisition' under the foreign subsidies screening will be broader than acquisition of control under the EUMR and will apply to 'acquisition – directly or indirectly – of at least [a specific percentage]% of the shares or voting rights or otherwise of "material influence" in an undertaking'.[132]

In order to assess whether a subsidized acquisition of an EU target results in a distortion of the internal market, the following criteria were proposed in the White Paper: (1) size the subsidy; (2) situation of the beneficiary; (3) situation on the markets concerned; (4) level of activity in the internal market of the parties concerned.[133] The established distortion could be then balanced against the positive impact that the investment may have within the EU or on public policy interests recognized by the EU.[134] These public

---

126 Ibid., Annex I.
127 Commission Notice on the notion of State aid as referred to in Article 107(1) of the Treaty on the Functioning of the European Union, OJ C262/1, 19 July 2016.
128 White Paper, Annex I.
129 Ibid., para 4.2.2.2. The EU target is defined as any undertaking established in the EU with significant presence measured at EUR 100 million or above in terms of annual turnover.
130 Ibid., para 4.2.1.
131 Ibid., para 4.2.2.2.
132 Ibid., para 4.2.2.1. See also Thomas Weck and Philipp Reinhold, 'Foreign Subsidies Regulation: Making Sense of the Commission's New White Paper' (Competition Policy International, 22 June 2020) <www.competitionpolicyinternational.com/foreign-subsidies-regulationmaking-sense-of-the-commissions-new-white-paper/> accessed 31 July 2020.
133 Ibid., para 4.2.3.
134 Ibid., para 4.2.4.

policy objectives, referred to as 'EU interest tests', may include creating jobs, achieving climate neutrality, protecting the environment, digital transformation, security, public order and public safety, and consumer interests.[135]

When discussing the institutional framework for the EU screening of foreign subsidies, the Commission proposed that for the sake of consistency and expediency of enforcement, the Commission could be made exclusively responsible for *ex ante* review of the notified acquisitions because 'such a system would ensure a one-stop-shop control across the EU for acquisitions above certain thresholds and avoid that for a single subsidized acquisition companies may have to deal with several Member State authorities at the same time'.[136] As a result, the foreign subsidies screening may be dealt by the Commission in parallel with the merger assessment if the notified acquisition also reaches the 'Community dimension' threshold under the EUMR.[137] There also may be an overlap between the EU FDI Screening Regulation and the foreign subsidies screening 'if a foreign direct investment constitutes an acquisition that is facilitated by a foreign subsidy and raises concerns with regard to security and public order'.[138] In that case, the foreign subsidies screening carried out by the Commission would run in parallel with the FDI screening on security grounds carried out by the competent authorities of the Member States under the EU FDI Screening Regulation.

Bibliography

Blachucki M, 'Public Interest Considerations in Merger Control Assessment' (2014) 35 *European Competition Law Review* 380.

Bradford A, RJ Jackson Jr., J Zytnick, 'Is E.U. Merger Control Used for Protectionism? An Empirical Analysis' (2018) 15 *Journal of Empirical Legal Studies* 165.

Budzinski O, A Stöhr, 'Public Interest Considerations in European Merger Control Regimes' (2019) 25 *Ilmenau Economics Discussion Papers No. 13* <www.econstor.eu/bitstream/10419/203144/1/1671887840.pdf> accessed 31 July 2020.

Cuadrado EZ, 'The EU Commission Decides Not to Formally Intervene Following a Claim by Banks Bidding to Merge That the Italian Banking Regulator Created Obstacles to Their Respective Bids (BBVA/ABN)' (2005) *e-Competitions* April 2005, Art. N° 36756 <www.concurrences.com/en/bulletin/news-issues/april-2005/The-European-Commission-decides-36756> accessed 31 July 2020.

Di Falco C, 'Italy: COVID-19 Crisis Inspires Global Tightening of Foreign Investment Screening' (Norton Rose Fulbright, 12 May 2020) <www.nortonrosefulbright.com/en/knowledge/publications/503220b7/italy> accessed 27 July 2020.

---

135 Ibid., para 4.1.4.
136 Ibid., para 4.2.7.
137 Ibid., para 6.1.
138 Ibid., para 6.7.

Elliott P, 'The EU Commission Prohibits a Merger in the Market for Railway Signalling and Very High-Speed Trains (Siemens/Alstom)' (2019) *e-Competitions* February 2019, Art. N° 89603 <www.concurrences.com/en/bulletin/news-issues/february-2019/the-eu-commission-prohibits-a-merger-in-the-market-for-railway-signalling-and-89603> accessed 31 July 2020.

García Fernández C, M Troncoso Ferrer, S Moya Izquierdo, 'The EU Commission Prohibits a Merger in the Market for Railway Signalling and Very High-Speed Trains (Siemens/Alstom)' (2019) *e-Competitions* February 2019, Art. N° 89741 <www.concurrences.com/en/bulletin/news-issues/february-2019/the-eu-commission-prohibits-a-merger-in-the-market-for-railway-signalling-and-en> accessed 31 July 2020.

Heim M, 'How Can European Competition Law Address Market Distortions Caused by State-Owned Enterprises?' (2019) *Bruegel Policy Contribution No. 18* <www.bruegel.org/wp-content/uploads/2019/12/PC-18_2019-181219.pdf> accessed 31 July 2020.

Henry D, J Buhart, 'The EU Commission Prohibits a Merger in the Railway Sector and Reaffirms That Industrial Policy Objectives Have No Role to Play When It Comes to Applying the EU Merger Control Rules (Siemens/Alstom)' (2019) *e-Competitions* February 2019, Art. N° 89282 <www.concurrences.com/en/bulletin/news-issues/february-2019/the-eu-commission-prohibits-a-merger-in-the-railway-sector-and-reaffirms-that> accessed 31 July 2020.

Leonard M, others, 'Redefining Europe's Economic Sovereignty' (European Council on Foreign Relations, 2019) <www.ecfr.eu/publications/summary/redefining_europes_economic_sovereignty> accessed 31 July 2020.

Makela T, 'The EU Court of Justice Rules for the First Time on Article 21(3) of the Merger Regulation (Portuguese Republic/Commission)' (2004) *e-Competitions Judicial Review*, Art. N° 37325 <www.concurrences.com/en/bulletin/special-issues/judicial-review/mergers/the-european-court-of-justice-rules-for-the-first-time-on-article-21-3-of-the> accessed 31 July 2020.

Meunier S, 'Divide and Conquer? China and the Cacophony of Foreign Investment Rules in the EU' (2014) 21 *Journal of European Public Policy* 996.

Németh Z, 'The Hungarian Competition Authority Clears the Acquisition of the Prospective Owner and Operator of the Gas Interconnector between Slovakia and Hungary by Two State Owned Companies (Magyar Villamos Művek/MFB Invest Befektetési és Vagyonkezelő/Magyar Gáz Tranzit)' (2012) *e-Competitions* March 2012, Art. N° 49212 <www.concurrences.com/en/bulletin/news-issues/march-2012/the-hungarian-competition-authority-clears-the-acquisition-of-the-prospective-en> accessed 31 July 2020.

Nourry A, D Rabinowitz, 'European Champions: What Now for EU Merger Control after Siemens/Alstom?' (2020) 41 *European Competition Law Review* 116.

Oster T, F Leroux, J Witting, 'The EU Commission Prohibits a Merger in the Railway Sector (Siemens/Alstom)' (2019) *e-Competitions* February 2019, Art. N° 94671 <www.concurrences.com/en/bulletin/news-issues/february-2019/the-eu-commission-prohibits-a-merger-in-the-railway-sector-siemens-alstom> accessed 31 July 2020.

Pochart F, M Rauline, O de la Verteville, 'Compulsory Licenses Granted by Public Authorities: An Application in the Covid-19 Crisis in France? Part 1' (Kluwer

Patent Blog, 23 April 2020) <http://patentblog.kluweriplaw.com/2020/04/23/compulsory-licenses-granted-by-public-authorities-an-application-in-the-covid-19-crisis-in-france-part-1/?doing_wp_cron=15943681298.0947930812835693359375> accessed 31 July 2020.

Reins L, 'The European Union's Framework for FDI Screening: Towards an Ever More Growing Competence over Energy Policy?' (2019) 128 *Energy Policy* 665.

Röhling F, others, 'COVID-19: Shut Down Also for Foreign Direct Investments Into Europe? Commission Issues Guidance to Member States on How to Protect Strategic Assets' (Freshfields Bruckhaus Deringer, 27 March 2020) <https://transactions.freshfields.com/post/102g33i/covid-19-shut-down-also-for-foreign-direct-investments-into-europe-commission-i> accessed 31 July 2020.

Svetlicinii A, 'The Acquisitions of the Chinese State-Owned Enterprises under the National Merger Control Regimes of the EU Member States: Searching for a Coherent Approach' (2018) 2 *Market and Competition Law Review* 99.

Svetlicinii A, 'The Interactions of Competition Law and Investment Law: The Case of Chinese State-Owned Enterprises and EU Merger Control Regime', in Julien Chaisse, Leïla Choukroune and Sufian Jusoh (eds) *Handbook of International Investment Law and Policy* (Springer, 2019).

Weck T, P Reinhold, 'Foreign Subsidies Regulation: Making Sense of the Commission's New White Paper' (Competition Policy International, 22 June 2020) <www.competitionpolicyinternational.com/foreign-subsidies-regulationmaking-sense-of-the-commissions-new-white-paper/> accessed 31 July 2020.

Wong H, 'The Case for Compulsory Licensing during COVID-19' *Journal of Global Health* <www.jogh.org/documents/issue202001/jogh-10-010358.htm> accessed 31 July 2020.

Ye B, 'Comments on EU's Proposed Regulation on Establishing a European Framework for Screening FDI: Right Legal Basis?' (2018) 4 *EU-China Observer* 9.

Conclusion

Deng Xiaoping was famous for his saying that it doesn't matter whether a cat is black or white as long as it catches mice. The antitrust enforcer version of this saying should be that: it doesn't matter where the company comes from, as long as it competes – by the rules.[1]

The application of the EU merger control rules to the economic concentrations involving SOEs have been developed by the Commission in cases concerning companies from the EU/EEA markets, which are subjected to the regulatory environment of the EU law embracing the principle of competitive neutrality. In the EU, the SOEs do not have any specific regulatory treatment under the EUMR and their mergers and acquisitions have to pass through the same procedural steps and substantive assessment standards. As a result, the SOEs were regarded as 'undertakings', whereas the respective states and their authorities exercising ownership rights were treated as 'persons' under the EUMR. When appreciating the degree of control of coordination that particular states exert over the commercial conduct of their SOEs, the Commission engaged in a case-by-case determination of a 'single economic unit' that would encompass all undertakings effectively controlled by the single entity. In some cases, the Commission looked at the factual evidence showing whether a state or its entity facilitate coordination among its SOEs. In other cases, especially those involving foreign SOEs, the Commission considered a possibility of facilitating such coordination. The determinations of a 'single economic unit' allowed the Commission to estimate the relevant turnover of the 'undertakings concerned'

---

1 Margrethe Vestager, Enforcing Competition Rules in the Global Village, New York University (20 April 2015) https://wayback.archive-it.org/12090/20191129202144/https://ec.europa.eu/commission/commissioners/2014-2019/vestager/announcements/enforcing-competition-rules-global-village_en.

for the purpose of establishing the 'Community dimension' and asserting its authority under the EUMR. At the same time, these determinations played a relatively limited role in addressing the potential anti-competitive scenarios involving the coordination among the SOEs owned by the same state. Although the merger cases involving non-controlling state shareholdings, discussed in Chapter 1, also demonstrated the ability of the state to exert decisive influence on the market conduct of its SOEs, this issue did not receive an in-depth consideration in the merger assessments carried out by the Commission.

Although in other countries the SOEs may bear important social functions by producing the essential goods and services and offering employment and social protection within the respective societies, in China the SOEs remain as one of the pillars of the 'socialism with Chinese characteristics'. The dominance of the SOEs on many domestic markets and their indispensable role in the implementation of the industrial policies such as Made in China 2025 and the Belt and Road Initiative have conditioned special attention to the effective control and operational efficiency of the Chinese SOEs. As discussed in Chapter 2, the strengthening of the Chinese State's control over its SOEs became especially apparent after 2015, when the deepening of the SOE reform resulted in experimentation with the new forms of ownership-based and non-ownership control over its SOEs. The two forms of control have developed in parallel: the State Council operating through the Central SASAC as a state majority shareholder and the CPC-led personnel appointments and party branches within the SOEs overseeing the work of the SOE executives and ensuring their adherence to the implementation of the state policies. The analysis of the Chinese merger control enforcement by the MOFCOM (and later by the SAMR) in cases involving centrally controlled SOEs also confirms that the industrial policy pursuing the consolidation of the SOE sectors prevails over competition protection objectives of the AML.

The ongoing SOE reform in China combined with the consolidation of the SOE sector and 'go global' policy encouraging outward FDI have increased the presence of the Chinese SOEs on the global markets though international trade and investment. The growing turnovers of the Chinese SOEs in the European markets have triggered the notification of the acquisitions under the EUMR. Chapter 3 discussed how the European Commission has attempted to define a 'single economic unit' in cases involving Chinese SOEs. With the exception of the *EDF/CGN/NNB* merger, where a wider 'single economic unit' would trigger the notification obligation under the EUMR, the Commission has opted for an open-ended and case-by-case 'wait and see' approach to the exact scope of the 'single economic unit' including Chinese SOEs. The EU has definitely 'awakened to the challenge but it has not yet defined its response. It needs to shape a strategy for its foreign policy, its technology and investment policy on China in third markets and multilateral institutions'.[2] Following the string of clearances of the Chinese SOE acquisitions in Europe contrasted with the Commission's blocking of the *Siemens/Alstom* merger, the calls for regulatory reform of the EU merger control rules have been voiced by numerous stakeholders.

Chapter 4 discussed the most prominent regulatory proposals for the reform of the EU merger control regime with the aim to make the latter more efficient in addressing the anti-competitive distortions on the EU internal market that may be triggered by the foreign SOE acquisitions. A series of the industrial policy proposals have urged the Commission to consider changing the existing merger control rules along the two major lines: (1) to attach more importance to the competitiveness of the European companies on the global market and relax the application of the merger control rules to allow the creation of the 'European champions'; (2) to take into account the state control and state support enjoyed by the foreign SOEs when assessing the likely effect of their acquisitions on the European markets. In a series of public statements, the Commission has indicated its unwillingness to deviate from the principle of non-discrimination embedded into the EUMR, which calls for an equal treatment of foreign and domestic, private and state owned companies. The Commission also resolutely rejected the attempts to introduce industrial policy considerations into the merger control assessment, which should be based exclusively on the merger's likely effect on competition.

Although the EU merger control rules remain unchanged, they do not affect the functioning of the national merger control regimes of the Member States. Without detailed guidance from the Commission or the ECN, the NCAs have developed their own assessment and interpretation tools applied in the SOE-related merger cases. The selective review of the merger decisions issued by the NCAs indicated a varying degree of attention attributed to the SOE status of the acquiring undertakings and the assessment of possible coordination of market conduct with other SOEs under the control of the same state. In this regard, the Commission should be encouraged to develop a detailed guidance on merger assessment of SOE-related concentrations. Such guidelines on 'SOE market distortions will allow the Commission to hone its analytical tools to the specific characteristics of SOEs and provide clarity to the market about where its enforcement priorities lie'.[3]

2 Mark Leonard and others, 'Redefining Europe's Economic Sovereignty' (European Council on Foreign Relations, 2019) <www.ecfr.eu/publications/summary/redefining_europes_eco nomic_sovereignty> accessed 31 July 2020, 4.
3 Mathew Heim, 'How Can European Competition Law Address Market Distortions Caused by State-Owned Enterprises?' (2019) *Bruegel Policy Contribution No. 18* <www.bruegel. org/wp-content/uploads/2019/12/PC-18_2019-181219.pdf> accessed 31 July 2020, 7.

Although the reform of the EU merger control seems to be off the table for the Commission, an important regulatory development in the field of investment law – the EU FDI Screening Regulation – has been adopted and entered into force. Although the ultimate power of decision concerning the approval/prohibition of FDI on the grounds of public security and public order remains with the Member States, it was widely anticipated that new and more detailed FDI screening rules will be adopted at the national level, which will add another level of regulatory scrutiny for Chinese SOEs' future acquisitions on the European markets. The economic disruptions and volatility of the stock markets caused by the COVID-19 pandemic will further accelerate the adoption of the new foreign investment restrictions by the Member States. Furthermore, the Commission's White Paper on foreign subsidies revealed the proposal to adopt an additional regulatory screening for acquisitions that have been facilitated by financial contributions of non-EU states. Together with the merger control and the FDI screening on grounds of public policy, the new instrument that is expected to be adopted in 2021 will introduce a third regulatory framework that will be applied to the future SOE acquisitions in the EU.

Annexes

Annex 1

Chinese state owned enterprises

Table 1 SOEs controlled by the Central SASAC[1]

No.	Name (English)	Chinese language website	English language website
1	China National Nuclear Corporation (CNNC)	www.cnnc.com.cn/	http://en.cnnc.com.cn/index.html
2	China Aerospace Science and Technology Corporation (CASC)	www.spacechina.com/n25/index.html	http://english.spacechina.com/n16421/index.html
3	China Aerospace Science and Industry Corporation (CASIC)	www.casic.com.cn/	www.casic.com/
4	Aviation Industry Corporation of China (AVIC)	www.avic.com.cn/	www.avic.com/en/
5	China State Shipbuilding Corporation	www.csic.com.cn/index.html	–
6	China North Industries Group Corporation (Norinco Group)	www.norincogroup.com.cn/	http://en.norincogroup.com.cn/
7	China South Industries Group Corporation (CSGC)	www.csgc.com.cn	www.csgc.com.cn/g1280.aspx
8	China Electronics Technology Group Corporation (CETC)	www.cetc.com.cn/	http://en.cetc.com.cn/
9	Aero Engine Corporation of China (AECC)	www.aecc.cn/	–
10	China Rongtong Asset Management Group	–	–
11	China National Petroleum Corporation (CNPC)	www.cnpc.com.cn/cnpc/index.shtml	www.cnpc.com.cn/en/
12	China Petrochemical Corporation (Sinopec)	www.sinopecgroup.com/group/	www.sinopecgroup.com/group/en/
13	China National Offshore Oil Corporation (CNOOC)	www.cnooc.com.cn/	www.cnooc.com.cn/col/col5191/index.html
14	National Petroleum & Natural Gas Pipeline Network Group	–	–
15	State Grid Corporation of China (SGCC)	www.sgcc.com.cn/	www.sgcc.com.cn/ywlm/index.shtml
16	China Southern Power Grid Corporation (CSG)	www.csg.cn/	http://eng.csg.cn/h5.html

(Continued)

1 The list of centrally controlled SOEs is maintained by SASAC at <www.sasac.gov.cn/n2588035/n2641579/n2641645/c4451749/content.html> accessed 31 July 2020.

Table 1 (Continued)

No.	Name (English)	Chinese language website	English language website
17	China HuaNeng Group (CHNG)	www.chng.com.cn/	www.chng.com.cn/eng
18	China DaTang Corporation (China-CDT)	www.china-cdt.com//indexAction.ndo?action=showindex	www.cccme.org.cn/shop/cccme8991/index.aspx
19	China HuaDian Corporation (CHD)	www.chd.com.cn/	http://eng.chd.com.cn/
20	State Power Investment Corporation (SPIC)	www.spic.com.cn/xdh/	http://eng.spic.com.cn/
21	China Three Gorges Corporation (CTG)	www.ctg.com.cn/	www.ctg.com.cn/en/
22	China Energy Investment Corporation (CEIC)	www.ceic.com/	www.ceic.com/ginyjtwwEn/index.shtml
23	China Telecommunications Corporation (China Telecom)	www.chinatelecom.com.cn/	www.chinatelecomglobal.com/
24	China United Network Communications Group (China Unicom)	www.chinaunicom.com.cn/	–
25	China Mobile Communications Group (China Mobile)	www.10086.cn/index_5074.htm	www.chinamobileltd.com/en/global/home.php
26	China Electronics Corporation (CEC)	www.cec.com.cn/	http://en.cec.com.cn/
27	China First Automobile Works Group (FAW)	www.faw.com.cn/	www.faw.com/
28	DongFeng Motor Corporation	www.dfmc.com.cn/	www.dongfeng-global.com/
29	China First Heavy Industries (CFHI)	www.cfhi.com/yzjt/index.html	www.cfhi.com/en/index.html
30	China National Machinery Industry Corporation (Sinomach)	www.sinomach.com.cn/	www.sinomach.com.cn/en/
31	Harbin Electric Corporation	www.harbin-electric.com/	http://en.harbin-electric.com/
32	DongFang Electric Corporation	www.dongfang.com/	www.dongfang.com.cn/
33	Ansteel Group Corporation (Ansteel)	www.ansteel.cn/	http://en.ansteel.cn/
34	China BaoWu Steel Group Corporation	www.baowugroup.com/	www.baowugroup.com/en/#
35	Aluminum Corporation of China (Chinalco)	www.chinalco.com.cn/zgly/index.htm	www.chalco.com.cn/chalcoen/index.htm
36	China COSCO Shipping Corporation	www.coscoshipping.com/	http://en.coscoshipping.com/
37	China National Aviation Holding Corporation (Air China)	www.airchina.com/	www.airchina.com.cn/en/index.shtml
38	China Eastern Air Holding Company (China Eastern)	www.ceair.com/	www.ceair.com
39	China Southern Air Holding Company (China Southern)	www.csair.cn/	www.csair.cn/csapen/index.html
40	SinoChem Group	www.sinochem.com/	http://english.sinochem.com/

42	China Minmetals Corporation	www.minmetals.com.cn/	www.minmetals.com/english/
43	China General Technology Group Holding	www.genertec.com.cn/default.aspx	
44	China State Construction Engineering Corporation (CSCEC)	www.cscec.com.cn/?lang=zh	https://english.cscec.com/
45	China Grain Reserves Group (Sinograin)	www.sinograin.com.cn/indexWeb.html	—
46	State Development & Investment Corporation (SDIC)	www.sdic.com.cn/cn/index.htm	www.sdic.com.cn/en/index.htm
47	China Merchants Group	www.cmhk.com/main/	www.cmhk.com/en/
48	China Resources Holdings	www.crc.com.hk/	http://en.crc.com.cn/
49	China Tourism Group	www.ctg.cn/index_2018/index.html	www.ctg.cn/en/index.htm
50	Commercial Aircraft Corporation of China (COMAC)	www.comac.cc/	http://english.comac.cc/
51	China Energy Conservation & Environmental Protection Group (CECEP)	www.cecep.cn/	www.en.cecep.cn/
52	China International Engineering Consulting Corporation (CIECC)	www.ciecc.com.cn/	http://en.ciecc.com.cn/
53	China ChengTong Holdings Group	www.cctgroup.com.cn/	www.cctgroup.com.cn/cctgroupen/index/index.html
54	China National Coal Group	www.chinacoal.com/	https://en.chinacoal.com/
55	China Coal Technology & Engineering Group (CCTEG)	www.ccteg.cn/	http://en.ccteg.cn/
56	China Academy of Machinery Science & Technology Group	www.cam.com.cn/	www.cam.com.cn/en/index.aspx
57	Sinosteel Corporation	www.sinosteel.com/	http://en.sinosteel.com/
58	China Iron & Steel Research Institute Group	www.cisri.com.cn/	www.cisri.com/english/tabid/520/language/zh-CN/Default.aspx
59	China National Chemical Corporation (ChemChina)	www.chemchina.com.cn/	www.chemchina.com.cn/en/index.htm
60	China National Chemical Engineering Group Corporation (CNCEC)	https://cncec.cn/	—
61	China National Salt Industry Corporation	www.chinasalt.com.cn/	www.chinasalt.com.cn/english/
62	China National Building Materials Group (CNBM)	www.cnbm.com.cn/	www.cnbm.com.cn/EN/

(*Continued*)

Table 1 (Continued)

No.	Name (English)	Chinese language website	English language website
63	China Nonferrous Metal Mining Group (CNMC)	www.cnmc.com.cn/	www.cnmc.com.cn/indexen.jsp
64	General Research Institute for Nonferrous Metals Group (GRINM)	www.grinm.com/	www.grinm.com/Default.aspx?alias=www.grinm.com/english
65	Beijing General Research Institute of Mining & Metallurgy Technology Group (BGRIMM)	www.bgrimm.com	http://english.bgrimm.com
66	China International Intellectech Company	www.ciic.com.cn/	—
67	China Academy of Building Research	www.cabr.com.cn/	www.cabr.com.cn/engweb/index.htm
68	China Railway Rolling Stock Corporation (CRRC)	www.crrcgc.cc/	www.crrcgc.cc/en
69	China Railway Signal & Communication Group (CRSC)	www.crsc.cn/	www.crsc.cn/6928.html
70	China Railway Group	www.crecg.com/	www.crecg.com/english/index.html
71	China Railway Construction Corporation	www.crcc.cn/	http://english.crcc.cn/
72	China Communications Construction Company	www.ccccltd.cn/	http://en.ccccltd.cn/
73	Potevio Group Corporation	www.potevio.com/	—
74	China Information & Communications Technologies Group Corporation (CICT)	www.cict.com	—
75	China National Agricultural Development Group	www.cnadc.com.cn/	www.cnadc.com.cn/en/index.jhtml
76	China Forestry Group Corporation	www.cfgc.cn/	http://en.cfgc.cn/
77	China National Pharmaceutical Group Corporation (Sinopharm)	www.sinopharm.com/	www.sinopharm.com/en/1156.html
78	China Poly Group Corporation	www.poly.com.cn/	www.poly.com.cn/english/1627.html
79	China Architecture Design & Research Group	www.cadreg.com.cn/	http://en.cadreg.com/
80	China Metallurgical Geology Bureau (CMGB)	www.cmgb.com.cn/	www.cmgb.com.cn/en/974536/index.html
81	China National Administration of Coal Geology	www.ccgc.cn/	www.ccgc.cn/col/col522/index.html
82	Xinxing Cathay International Group	www.xxcig.com/	http://english.xxcig.com/
83	China TravelSky Holding Company	—	—
84	China National Aviation Fuel Group	www.cnaf.com/	www.cnaf.com/english.html

85	China Aviation Supplies Holding Company	www.casc.com.cn/cas/	www.casc.com.cn/cas/en/
86	Power Construction Corporation of China (PowerChina)	www.powerchina.cn/	https://en.powerchina.cn//
87	China Energy Engineering Group (Energy China)	www.ceec.net.cn/	http://en.ceec.net.cn/
88	China Anneng Construction Group	—	—
89	China National Gold Group	www.chinagoldgroup.com/	—
90	China General Nuclear Power Corporation (CGN)	www.cgnpc.com.cn/	http://en.cgnpc.com.cn/
91	China Hualu Group	www.hualu.com.cn/	www.hualu.com.cn/en/
92	Overseas Chinese City Group (OCT)	www.chinaoct.com/	—
93	Nam Kwong (Group) Company	www.namkwong.com.mo/	http://en.namkwong.com.mo/
94	China XD Group	www.xd.com.cn/	www.xd.com.cn/
95	China Railway Materials Group	www.crmsc.com.cn/	—
96	China Reform Holdings Corporation	www.crhc.cn/	—
97	China Certification and Inspection Group	www.ccic.com/	—

Table 2 Financial and banking SOEs

No.	Name	Controlling shareholder	Website
1	Central Huijin Investment Ltd.	China Investment Corporation (CIC)	www.huijin-inv.cn/en/
2	China Investment Corporation	State Council	www.china-inv.cn/en/
3	China Development Bank	Ministry of Finance	www.cdb.com.cn/English/
4	The Export-Import Bank of China	State Council	www.eximbank.gov.cn/
5	Agricultural Development Bank of China	State Council	www.adbc.com.cn/en/index.html
6	Industrial and Commercial Bank of China	Ministry of Finance and Central Huijin Investment Ltd.	www.icbc-ltd.com/icbcltd/en/
7	Agricultural Bank of China	Ministry of Finance and Central Huijin Investment Ltd.	www.abchina.com/en/
8	Bank of China	Central Huijin Investment Ltd.	www.boc.cn/en/
9	China Construction Bank	Central Huijin Investment Ltd.	www.ccb.com/en/home/indexv3.html
10	Bank of Communications	Ministry of Finance	www.bankcomm.com/BankCommSite/shtml/jyir/en/2600212/list.shtml?channelId=2600212
11	CITIC Group	State Council	www.group.citic/en/
12	China Everbright Group	Central Huijin Investment Ltd.	www.ebchina.com/ebchina/index/index.html
13	People's Insurance Company of China (PICC)	Ministry of Finance	www.picc.com/jtzzgx/en/
14	China Life Insurance Group	State Council	www.e-chinalife.com/IRchannel/Http/en/index.html
15	China Taiping Insurance Group	Ministry of Finance	https://en.cntaiping.com/
16	China Export & Credit Insurance Corporation	Central Huijin Investment Ltd.	www.sinosure.com.cn/en/
17	China Cinda Asset Management	Ministry of Finance	www.cinda.com.cn/en/investor/company/list.shtml
18	China Huarong Asset Management	Ministry of Finance	www.chamc.com.cn/en/
19	China Great Wall Asset Management	Ministry of Finance	www.gwamcc.com

20	China Orient Asset Management	Ministry of Finance	www.coamc.com
21	China Jianyin Investment	Central Huijin Investment Ltd.	www.jic.cn/
22	China Reinsurance Group	Central Huijin Investment Ltd.	http://eng.chinare.com.cn/
23	China Insurance Security Fund	Ministry of Finance	www.cisf.cn:8088/index.jsp
24	China Credit Trust	People's Insurance Company of China	www.cctic.com.cn
25	China Central Depository & Clearing	State Council	www.ccdc.com.cn/ccdc/en/index/index.shtml
26	China Galaxy Financial Holding Company	Central Huijin Investment Ltd.	www.china-galaxy.com.cn
27	China Securities Investor Protection Fund Corporation	State Council	www.sipf.com.cn/NewEN/aboutsipf/corporateprofile/index.shtml
28	China Securities Depository and Clearing Corporation Limited	Shanghai Stock Exchange, Shenzhen Stock Exchange	www.chinaclear.cn/english/About/about_index.shtml

Table 3 Other SOEs controlled by the State Council

No.	Name	Controlling entity	Website
1	China Publishing Group Corporation	State Council	http://en.cnpubg.com/
2	China State Railway Group	State Council	www.china-railway.com.cn/
3	China National Tobacco Corporation	State Council	www.tobacco.gov.cn/html/index.html
4	China Post Group	State Council	http://english.chinapost.com.cn/
5	China Arts and Entertainment Group (CAEG)	State Council	http://en.caeg.cn/

Annex II

Merger cases involving Chinese SOEs notified to the European Commission under the EU Merger Regulation[2]

Date of decision	Case identifier	Merging parties (SOE in bold)	Relevant market	Type of procedure
16/07/2004	COMP/M.3505	**TCL**/Alcatel	mobile handsets	6(1)(b) non-opposition
23/04/2007	COMP/M.4286	**China Shipbuilding**/Mitsubishi/Wärtsilä/JV	shipbuilding	6(1)(b) non-opposition
09/07/2009	COMP/M.5513	KMG/**China National Petroleum Corporation**/MMG	exploration, extraction, and processing of crude oil and natural gas	6(1)(b) non-opposition
17/06/2010	COMP/M.5841	Cathay Pacific Airways/**Air China**/ACC	air cargo services	6(1)(b) non-opposition
01/07/2010	COMP/M.5789	Geely/**Daqing State Assets Operation Co**/Volvo Cars	automobiles	6(1)(b) non-opposition
13/12/2010	COMP/M.6017	APMT/DPW/**China Ocean Shipping Company**/**Qingdao Port Group**/**Qingdao Qianwan Container Terminal**	maritime shipping	6(1)(b) non-opposition
11/02/2011	COMP/M.6111	**China Huaneng Group**/OTPPB/Intergen	electricity generation	6(1)(b) non-opposition
21/03/2011	COMP/M.6120	APMT/PSA/**China Ocean Shipping Company**/**Dalian Port Company**/**Dalian Port Container Terminal**	maritime shipping	6(1)(b) non-opposition
21/03/2011	COMP/M.6142	**Aviation Industry Corporation of China**/Pacific Century Motors	steering products and halfshaft components for automotive vehicles	6(1)(b) non-opposition
31/03/2011	COMP/M.6082	**China National Bluestar**/Elkem	silicon and carbon products	6(1)(b) non-opposition
19/05/2011	COMP/M.6113	DSM/**Sinochem**/JV	pharmaceuticals	6(1)(b) non-opposition

(Continued)

2 European Commission, Merger cases, <https://ec.europa.eu/competition/elojade/isef/index.cfm?clear=1&policy_area_id=2> accessed 31 July 2020.

(Continued)

Date of decision	Case identifier	Merging parties (SOE in bold)	Relevant market	Type of procedure
03/10/2011	COMP/M.6141	**China National Agrochemical Corporation**/Koor Industries/Makhteshim Agan Industries	agrochemical products	6(1)(b) non-opposition
13/05/2011	COMP/M.6151	**PetroChina**/Ineos/JV	petroleum refineries	6(1)(b) non-opposition
02/12/2011	COMP/M.6235	Honeywell/**Sinochem**/JV	insulation materials	6(1)(b) non-opposition
28/09/2011	COMP/M.6337	**CITIC Dicastal Wheel Maufacturing**/KSM Castings	light metal (aluminum) castings	6(1)(b) non-opposition
24/02/2012	COMP/M.6461	TPV/Philips TV Business	color TVs	6(1)(b) non-opposition
16/11/2012	COMP/M.6700	Talisman/**Sinopec**/JV	exploration and production of petroleum in the UK North Sea	6(1)(b) non-opposition
07/12/2012	COMP/M.6715	**China National Offshore Oil Corporation**/Nexen	exploration, development, production and sale of crude oil and natural gas	6(1)(b) non-opposition
07/03/2013	COMP/M.6807	Mercuria Energy Asset Management/**Sinomart KTS Development**/Vesta Terminals	maritime terminals for storage of petroleum products and biodiesel	6(1)(b) non-opposition
08/05/2013	COMP/M.6860	Volvo/**Dongfeng**/JV	production of trucks, buses, engines, axles and transmissions	6(1)(b) non-opposition
13/12/2013	COMP/M.7066	**China National Oil & Gas Development Corporation**/Novatek/Total EPY/Yamal LNG	development and exploration of hydrocarbon raw materials	6(1)(b) non-opposition
25/06/2014	COMP/M.7244	**China Huaxin Post and Telecommunication Economy Development Center**/Alcatel-Lucent Enterprise Business	hardware and software for enterprise communications and network solutions	6(1)(b) non-opposition
15/07/2014	COMP/M.7169	**Weichai Power**/Kion Group	production of forklift trucks, warehouse handling equipment and	6(1)(b) non-opposition

25/09/2014	*China Oil and Foodstuffs Corporation/ Nidera*	agricultural commodities and bio-energy products	6(1)(b) non-opposition
12/09/2014	*China Oil and Foodstuffs Corporation/ Noble Agri*	agricultural commodities	6(1)(b) non-opposition
11/12/2014	COMP/M.7405	*Yanfeng/JCI Interiors Business*	automotive components	6(1)(b) non-opposition
17/03/2015	COMP/M.7504	*Carlyle/CITIC/Asiasat*	satellite communications services	6(1)(b) non-opposition
01/07/2015	COMP/M.7643	*China National Tyre & Rubber Co/Pirelli*	automobile tires	6(1)(b) non-opposition
14/09/2015	COMP/M.7709	*Bright Food Group/Invermik*	daily consumer products	6(1)(b) non-opposition
10/03/2016	COMP/M.7850	*EDF/China General Nuclear Power Group/ NNB*	nuclear energy	6(1)(b) non-opposition
15/03/2016	COMP/M.7911	*China National Chemical Equipment Co/ KM Group*	plastics and rubber processing machinery, tires	6(1)(b) non-opposition
09/09/2016	COMP/M.8169	*Verlinvest/China Resources Co/JV*	food & beverages products	6(1)(b) non-opposition
03/10/2016	COMP/M.8170	*ChemChina/Adama*	crop protection products	6(1)(b) non-opposition
05/04/2017	COMP/M.7962	*ChemChina/Syngenta*	crop protection products	8(2) conditional clearance
15/02/2017	COMP/M.8190	*Weichai/Kion*	production of forklift trucks, warehouse handling equipment and other industrial trucks	6(1)(b) non-opposition
10/05/2017	COMP/M.8384	*Carlyle/CITIC/McDonald's/McDonald's China*	restaurants	6(1)(b) non-opposition
18/05/2017	COMP/M.8411	*Safran Group/China Eastern Air Holding/ JV*	aircraft landing gear maintenance, repair and overhaul services	6(1)(b) non-opposition
01/08/2017	COMP/M.8422	*ChemChina/AKC*	chemical products	6(1)(b) non-opposition
12/09/2017	COMP/M.8513	*Infineon Technologies/SAIC Motor/JV*	automotive power semiconductors for hybrid and electric vehicles	6(1)(b) non-opposition

(Continued)

(Continued)

Date of decision	Case identifier	Merging parties (SOE in bold)	Relevant market	Type of procedure
18/09/2017	COMP/M.8554	**China Investment Corporation**/Logicor Business	logistics warehouse assets	6(1)(b) non-opposition
27/10/2017	COMP/M.8542	The Carlyle Group/CVC/**China Investment Corporation**/Engie E&P International	exploration and production of oil and natural gas	6(1)(b) non-opposition
05/12/2017	COMP/M.8594	**COSCO Shipping**/OOIL	deep-sea container line shipping	6(1)(b) non-opposition
12/06/2018	COMP/M.8903	**Beijing Hainachuan Automotive Parts Co**/Gestamp China/Manufacturing JV/Sales JV	automotive components	6(1)(b) non-opposition
29/10/2018	COMP/M.9075	Continental/**Sichuan Chengfei Integration Technology Corp/Jiangsu Jintan Hualuogeng Technology Development**/JV	battery systems for mild hybrid electric vehicles	6(1)(b) non-opposition
17/12/2018	COMP/M.9150	**China Reinsurance Group Corporation**/Chaucer	reinsurance	6(1)(b) non-opposition
21/12/2018	COMP/M.9187	Autolaunch/**Beijing Electric Vehicle Co**/JVs	engineering services, manufacturing and supplying blade electric passenger vehicles	6(1)(b) non-opposition
14/02/2019	COMP/M.9243	KKR/**China Resources**/Genesis Care	medical services	6(1)(b) non-opposition
10/05/2019	COMP/M.9296	Macquarie/**China Investment Corporation**/Allianz/Dalmore/INPP/Gas Distribution Business of National Grid	gas distribution networks	6(1)(b) non-opposition
22/10/2019	COMP/M.9552	BP/**China National Aviation Fuel Group**/CNAF Air BP General Aviation Fuel Company	aviation fuel	6(1)(b) non-opposition
30/03/2020	COMP/M.9742	**Sinopec Group**/Joint Stock Company Novatek/GazpromBank/Sinova Natural Gas Company	natural gas	6(1)(b) non-opposition

Annex III

Merger cases under Article 21(4) EUMR

Date of decision	Case identifier	Merging parties	Member State and its invoking authority	Public interest(s) invoked	Outcome
15/06/2000	COMP/M.1858	Thomson-CSF/Racal (II)	United Kingdom, Secretary of State for Defence	public security concerns relating to the confidentiality of sensitive information	recognized
23/04/2007	COMP/M.4561	GE/Smiths Aerospace Group	United Kingdom, Secretary of State for Defence	protection of sensitive information and compliance with public procurement	recognized
26/05/2004	COMP/M.3418	General Dynamics/Alvis	United Kingdom, Secretary of State for Defence	protection of sensitive information, technologies essential to national security	recognized
20/09/2004	COMP/M.3559	Finmeccanica/Augusta-Westland	United Kingdom, Secretary of State for Defence	confidentiality of sensitive information and to the maintenance of strategic capabilities	recognized
14/03/2005	COMP/M.3720	BAE Systems/AMS	United Kingdom, Secretary of State for Defence	confidentiality of sensitive information and naval capabilities	recognized
21/12/1995	IV/M.567	Lyonnaise des Eaux/Northumbrian Water	United Kingdom, Secretary of State for Trade and Industry	water supply regulations	recognized
27/01/1999	IV/M.1346	EDF/London Electricity	United Kingdom, Secretary of State for Trade and Industry	licensing of electricity companies	recognized

(Continued)

(Continued)

Date of decision	Case identifier	Merging parties	Member State and its invoking authority	Public interest(s) invoked	Outcome
21/12/2010	COMP/M.5932	*News Corp/BSkyB*	United Kingdom, Secretary of State for Business Innovation and Skills, Office of Communications	media plurality concerns	recognized
14/03/1994	IV/M.423	*Newspaper Publishing*	United Kingdom, Secretary of State for Culture, Media and Sport	media plurality concerns	recognized
07/04/2017	COMP/M.8354	*Sky/Twenty-First Century Fox*	United Kingdom, Secretary of State for Culture, Media and Sport, Office of Communications	media plurality concerns	recognized
18/06/1996	IV/M.759	*Sun Alliance/Royal Insurance*	United Kingdom, Secretary of State for Trade and Industry	prudential rules	recognized
03/08/1999	IV/M.1616	*BSCH/A.de S. Champalimaud*	Portugal, Finance Minister	strategic sector for the national economy	refused
11/01/2001	COMP/M.2054	*Secil/Holderbank/ Cimpor*	Portugal, Finance Minister	national economic interests in privatization	refused
18/10/2005	COMP/M.3894	*UniCredito/HVB*	Poland, State Treasury	national economic interests in privatization	refused
22/09/2006	COMP/M.4249	*Abertis/Autostrade*	Italy, Minister for Infrastructure	investment capacity and security standards	refused
27/04/2005	COMP/M.3768	*BBVA/BNL*	Italy, Bank of Italy	national economic security in banking sector	refused
27/04/2005	COMP/M.3780	*ABN AMRO/Banca Antonveneta*	Italy, Bank of Italy	national economic security in banking sector	refused
25/04/2006	COMP/M.4197	*E.ON/Endesa*	Spain, Council of Ministers	security of energy supply	refused
05/07/2007	COMP/M.4685	*Enel/Acciona/Endesa*	Spain, Minister of Industry, Tourism and Trade	security of energy supply	refused

Annex IV

List of FDI screening mechanisms notified by the Member States (as of 28 July 2020)[3]

Member State	National legislation	Web link to full text
Austria	Foreign Commerce Act of 2011 (Section 25a)	German: www.ris.bka.gv.at/GeltendeFassung.wxe?Abfrage=Bundesnormen&Gesetzesnummer=20007221 English: https://trade.ec.europa.eu/doclib/docs/2019/june/tradoc_157940.pdf
Austria	Investment Control Act and amendments of the Foreign Commerce Act	German: www.ris.bka.gv.at/eli/bgbl/I/2020/87/20200724
Denmark	Act on War Material (The Danish Consolidated Act No. 1004 of 22 October 2012)	Danish: www.retsinformation.dk/eli/lta/2012/1004
Denmark	Act on the Continental Shelf and Certain Pipelines Installations on Territorial Waters (The Danish Consolidated Act No. 1189 of 21 September 2018)	Danish: www.retsinformation.dk/eli/lta/2018/1189
Finland	Act on the Screening of Foreign Corporate Acquisitions (172/2012)	Finnish: www.finlex.fi/fi/laki/ajantasa/2012/20120172 Swedish: www.finlex.fi/sv/laki/ajantasa/2012/20120172 English: https://trade.ec.europa.eu/doclib/docs/2019/june/tradoc_157939.pdf
Finland	Act on Transfers of Real Estate Property Requiring Special Permission (470/2019)	Finnish: www.finlex.fi/fi/laki/alkup/2019/20190470 Swedish: www.finlex.fi/sv/laki/alkup/2019/20190470
France	Financial and Monetary Code Legal Section Book I Title V: Financial ealings with Foreign Countries, Articles L.151–1 to L.151–7	English: https://trade.ec.europa.eu/doclib/docs/2020/march/tradoc_158692.pdf

(*Continued*)

3 EU Commission, <https://trade.ec.europa.eu/doclib/docs/2019/june/tradoc_157946.pdf> accessed 31 July 2020.

(Continued)

Member State	National legislation	Web link to full text
France	Financial and Monetary Code Legal Section Book I Title V: Financial Dealings with Foreign Countries, Articles R.151–1 to L.151–18	English: https://trade.ec.europa.eu/doclib/docs/2020/march/tradoc_158692.pdf
France	Order of 31 December 2019 relating to foreign investments in France	English: https://trade.ec.europa.eu/doclib/docs/2020/march/tradoc_158692.pdf
France	French Commercial Code Article L.233–3, Article L.430–1	English: https://trade.ec.europa.eu/doclib/docs/2020/march/tradoc_158692.pdf
France	Article 459 of the Customs Code (penal sanctions)	French: www.legifrance.gouv.fr/affichCodeArticle.do?idArticle=LEGIARTI000025092487&cidTexte=LEGITEXT000006071570&dateTexte=20190426&oldAction=rechCodeArticle&fastReqId=1565183568&nbResultRech=1
Germany	Foreign Trade and Payments Act of 6 June 2013 (Federal Law Gazette, part I p. 1482) as last amended by Article 4 of the Act of 20 July 2017 (Federal Law Gazette, part I p. 2789	German: www.gesetze-im-internet.de/awg_2013/ English: www.gesetze-im-internet.de/englisch_awg/
Germany	Foreign Trade and Payments Ordinance of 2 August 2013 (Federal Law Gazette part I p. 2865), as last amended by Article 1 pf the Ordinance of 19 December 2018	German: www.gesetze-im-internet.de/awv_2013/ English: www.gesetze-im-internet.de/englisch_awv/
Hungary	Act LVII of 2018 on Controlling Foreign Investments Violating Hungary's Security Interests	Hungarian: www.kozlonyok.hu/nkonline/MKPDF/hiteles/MK18157.pdf English: https://trade.ec.europa.eu/doclib/docs/2019/june/tradoc_157938.pdf
Hungary	Government Decree 246/2018. (XII. 17.) on the Implementation of Act LVII of 2018 on Controlling Foreign Investments Violating Hungary's Security Interests	Hungarian: www.kozlonyok.hu/nkonline/MKPDF/hiteles/MK18201.pdf English: https://trade.ec.europa.eu/doclib/docs/2020/july/tradoc_158835.pdf

Hungary	Act LVIII of 2020 on the Transitional Rules Related to the End of the State of Danger and Pandemic Preparedness (section 85, paragraphs 276–292)	Hungarian: https://trade.ec.europa.eu/doclib/docs/2020/july/tradoc_158831.pdf English: https://trade.ec.europa.eu/doclib/docs/2020/july/tradoc_158832.pdf
Hungary	Government Decree 289/2020 (VI. 17.) defining the measures required for the economic protection of companies having their seats in Hungary	Hungarian: https://trade.ec.europa.eu/doclib/docs/2020/july/tradoc_158833.pdf English: https://trade.ec.europa.eu/doclib/docs/2020/july/tradoc_158834.pdf
Italy	Decree-law 15 March 2012, nr. 21 'Rules on special powers on corporate assets in the defense and national security sectors, as well as for activities of strategic importance in the energy, transport and communications sectors'	Italian: www.normattiva.it/uri-res/N2Ls?urn:nir:stato:decreto.legge:2012-03-15;21!vig=
Italy	Amendments to the regulation on special powers in sectors of strategic importance set forth in Articles 3 and 4-bis of the Decree-law 21 September 2019, nr. 105, converted with amendments by law November 18, 2019, nr. 133	Italian: www.gazzettaufficiale.it/eli/gu/2019/11/20/272/sg/pdf
Italy	Decree-Law 8 April 2020, nr. 23 'Urgent measures regarding access to credit and tax obligations for businesses, special powers in strategic sectors, as well as interventions in the field of health and labour, extension of administrative and procedural terms'. Articles 15–16	Italian: www.gazzettaufficiale.it/eli/gu/2020/04/08/94/sg/pdf
Italy	Decree of the President of the Republic 19 February 2014, nr. 35 'Regulation for the identification of procedures for the activation of special powers in the fields of defense and national security, pursuant to article 1, paragraph 8, of the decree-law 15 March 2012, nr. 21'	Italian: www.normattiva.it/uri-res/N2Ls?urn:nir:stato:decreto.del.presidente.della.repubblica:2014-02-19;35!vig=

(Continued)

(Continued)

Member State	National legislation	Web link to full text
Italy	Decree of the President of the Republic 25 March 2014, nr. 86 'Regulation for the identification of procedures for the activation of special powers in the energy, transport and communications sectors, pursuant to article 2, paragraph 9, of the decree-law 15 March 2012, nr. 21'	Italian: www.normattiva.it/uri-res/N2Ls?urn:nir:stato:decreto.del.presidente.della.repubblica:2014-03-25;86!vig=
Italy	Decree of the President of the Republic 25 March 2014, nr. 85 'Regulation for the identification of strategically important assets in the energy, transport and communications sectors, pursuant to article 2, paragraph 1, of Decree-Law 15 March 2012, nr. 21'	Italian: www.normattiva.it/uri-res/N2Ls?urn:nir:stato:decreto.del.presidente.della.repubblica:2014-03-25;85!vig=
Italy	Decree of the President of the Council of Ministers 6 June 2014, nr. 108 'Regulation for the identification of activities of strategic importance for the national defense and security system, pursuant to article 1, paragraph 1, of the decree-law 15 March 2012, nr. 21'	Italian: www.normattiva.it/uri-res/N2Ls?urn:nir:stato:decreto.del.presidente.del.consiglio.dei.ministri:2014-06-06;108!vig=
Italy	Decree of the President of the Council of Ministers 6 August 2014 'Identification of the organizational and procedural methods for carrying out the activities preparatory to the exercise of special powers'	Italian: www.governo.it/sites/governo.it/files/Dpcm_20140806_GP.pdf
Latvia	National Security Law, Chapter VI – Restrictions Ministry of Economy on Commercial Companies of Significance to National Security	Latvian: https://likumi.lv/doc.php?id=14011 English: https://likumi.lv/ta/en/id/14011-national-security-law

Country		
Lithuania	The Law on Protection of Objects Important to Ensuring National Security of the Republic of Lithuania, No. IX-1132 (new edition No. XIII-992 of 12 January 2018)	Lithuanian: www.e-tar.lt/portal/lt/legalAct/TAR.57E0E8B29108/asr
Lithuania	Resolution on the Rules of Procedure of the Commission approved by the Government, No. 1540 (new edition No. 266 of 21 March 2018)	Lithuanian: www.e-tar.lt/portal/lt/legalAct/TAR.31D2751BF93D/asr
Lithuania	Resolution on the Determination of the Protection Zones of Importance to National Security approved by the Government, No. 1252 (new edition No. 746 of 25 July 2018)	Lithuanian: www.e-tar.lt/portal/lt/legalActEditions/1350b4606e5111e4942895da095d8b69?faces-redirect=true
Lithuania	The Law on the Protection of Objects of Importance to Ensuring National Security, No. XIII-3257	Lithuanian: www.e-tar.lt/portal/lt/legalAct/0fe3e670c66211ea997c9ee767e856b4
Netherlands	Electricity Act 1998 (article 86f)	Dutch: https://wetten.overheid.nl/BWBR0009755/2019-01-01
Netherlands	Gas Act (article 66e)	Dutch: https://wetten.overheid.nl/BWBR0011440/2019-01-01
Netherlands	Ministerial Regulation Regarding the Notification of Change of Control Electricity Act 1998 and Gas Act	Dutch: https://wetten.overheid.nl/BWBR0032058/2012-10-09
Poland	Act of 24 July 2015 on Control of Certain Investments	Polish: http://prawo.sejm.gov.pl/isap.nsf/DocDetails.xsp?id=WDU20150001272
Poland	Regulation of Council of Ministers of 27 September 2018 on the List of Entities Subject to Protection	Polish: http://isap.sejm.gov.pl/isap.nsf/DocDetails.xsp?id=WDU20180002524
Portugal	Decree-Law no. 138/2014, of 15 September, published in the DR no 177, series I, on 15 September 2014	Portuguese: https://dre.pt/web/guest/pesquisa/-/search/56819089/details/maximized
Romania	Law of Competition 21 of 10 April 1996 republished and amended, Art. 47 (9)-(12)	Romanian: www.consiliulconcurentei.ro/uploads/docs/items/bucket8/id8047/lege_nr21_1996_actualizata_20160303.pdf English: www.consiliulconcurentei.ro/uploads/docs/concurenta/LEGEA_CONCURENTEI_Nr_21_eng_rev_1.pdf
Spain	Royal Decree 137/1993, which approves the regulation on weapons	Spanish: www.boe.es/eli/es/rd/1993/01/29/137

(Continued)

(Continued)

Member State	National legislation	Web link to full text
Spain	Royal Decree 664/99, on foreign investment	Spanish: www.boe.es/buscar/doc.php?id=BOE-A-1999-9938
Spain	Law 19/2003, on the legal system on transfers of capitals and foreign economic transactions and specific measures for the prevention of money laundering	Spanish: www.boe.es/eli/es/l/2003/07/04/19
Spain	Royal Decree-Law 8/2020, on urgent extraordinary measures to address the economic and social impact of COVID-19	Spanish: www.boe.es/buscar/doc.php?id=BOE-A-2020-3824
Spain	Royal Decree Law 11/2020, on urgent extraordinary measures to address the economic and social impact of COVID-19	Spanish: www.boe.es/buscar/doc.php?id=BOE-A-2020-4208
Spain	Law 7/2010, General Law on audiovisual communication	Spanish: www.boe.es/eli/es/l/2010/03/31/7/con
Spain	Law 3/2013, creating the National Commission on Markets and Competition	Spanish: www.boe.es/eli/es/l/2013/06/04/3
Spain	Law 9/2014 on Telecommunications	Spanish: www.boe.es/eli/es/l/2014/05/09/9/con

Index

Note: Page numbers in **bold** indicate a table on the corresponding page.

Printed in the United States
by Baker & Taylor Publisher Services